Silappadikaram

Manimekalai

Other books in this series

In Worship of Shiva
The Ramayana
The Mahabharata
Hymns of Guru Nanak
Legends of Devi

Silappadikaram
Manimekalai

Lakshmi Holmström

Illustrations by
A.V. Ilango

Sangam Books

Sangam Books Limited
57 London Fruit Exchange
Brushfield Street
London E1 6EP

By arrangement with
Orient Longman Limited
3-6-272, Himayatnagar
Hyderabad 500 029 (A.P.) INDIA

© Orient Longman Limited 1996

Published by
Sangam Books Limited 1996

The text of *Silappadikaram* is
adapted from the original *Kannagi* published
by Orient Longman in 1980

ISBN 0 86311 673 6

A catalogue record for this book is available from the British Library

Book Design : Orient Longman Ltd.

Phototypeset in Sabon by Venture Graphics Pvt. Ltd.
36 McNichols Road, Chetpet, Madras 600 031

Text printed in India at Indcom Press
West Mambalam, Madras 600 033

Colour plates printed in India at NPT Offset (P) Ltd.
Royapettah, Madras 600 014

Contents

Silappadikaram

Manimekalai

Colour Plates

For
Radhika and Savitri
and
with thanks to
Mark
Nalini
Thambi

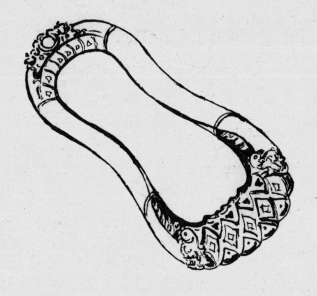

Silappadikaram

The three kingdoms

- Venkadam

Chera

Vanji

River Kaveri

Chola

- Kaveri-puum-pattinam
(Puhar)

Bay
of
Bengal

River Perujar

Madurai -

Pandya

River Vaigai

Arabian

Sea

- Korkai

Lanka

Kumari

1

A Wedding in Puhar

Let us praise the moon, let us praise the moon.
Like the cool white umbrella of our King
Whose garland is dusted with pollen,
It watches over this wide and beautiful earth.

Let us praise the sun, let us praise the sun.
Because it is like the royal discus
Of the King of the Kaveri lands,
Ever circling the golden summit of the sacred Meru mountain.

Let us praise the rain, let us praise the rain.
For it is like our King's generosity,
Standing on high and showering down
Upon this sea-enclosed land.

Let us praise Puhar, our beautiful Puhar.
For its fame is entwined always
With the glorious lineage of its Kings
And spreads to the sea-fences of this earth.

Kovalan was walking along the sea-front of Puhar, looking at
the ships at harbour. His father's agent, with whom he had
been sent, was talking to the captain of the small coastal craft
that had come in that morning from Korkai, centre of pearl fishery.
His father, Masattuvan, wealthiest of pearl merchants in Puhar,
owned a few small ships which travelled along the coast from Puhar
to Korkai and Musiri. But he owned bigger ships too, made of lashed
timber and carrying great sails. These went to fabled places with
haunting names — to Nagapuram in Java, to Kalakam in Burma,
and to Lanka. Those were the ships that Kovalan liked to pick out,
standing among the many vessels in the harbour. He was still young
enough to be thrilled by stories of adventures at sea, of pirates and

ship-wrecks, in which only the intervention of the goddess of their clan, the Goddess of the Sea, Manimekalai, had saved his ancestors.

Beyond the harbour, the water lay smooth, glinting in the sun like his mother's polished mirrors. The river Kaveri entered the eastern seas at this point, making an estuary so deep and wide, a harbour so safe, that Kovalan could see, even now, a great merchant ship coming into port without lowering its sail. It must be a Yavana ship from distant western lands. Decks of oars slapped smoothly, rhythmically in the water which was rippling now. Foam lashed against the sides of the ship. Soon it would be at the pier. Kovalan could see the crew, tall light-skinned foreigners. They were calling out to the porters on shore in their meagre and harsh-sounding Tamil. The porters were beginning to shout too as they got their ropes ready and cleared the way, for they would carry the goods that were landed into the warehouses just beyond the beach, where the bales must first be stamped with the tiger stamp of King Karikala.

Kovalan wondered what the foreigners had brought. There were usually amphoras of fine wine, and sometimes thorough-bred horses, but mostly various fancy goods, vases and lamps; the Yavanas came to buy rather than sell. He thought, though, that he would like to buy one of those Yavana lamps made in the shape of a woman who held between her hands the shallow receptacle in which oil and wick were placed. For Kannagi.

Kovalan smiled and remembered. With his usual tact, Masattuvan had said this morning that since his son was now adept at grading pearls, it was time he learnt about the trading end of the business. Would he care to go down to the port to meet the boats coming from Korkai? With equal tact Kovalan had gone with the agent. But he knew that his father wanted to be alone in order to talk to his old friend Manaykan who would be coming in later that morning. The two men would be discussing their children's wedding even now — his and Kannagi's.

He walked back along the sea-front, past those tall warehouses with curiously-shaped windows like deer's eyes, past the vendors of perfumes and pastes and flowers. He always enjoyed the port, the Maruvurpakkam of Puhar, so much. But he could not linger now. He joined the agent and tried to take an intelligent interest in the current price of pearls.

In the days of King Karikala the Great, most famous of the Chola Kings, Puhar was both capital and chief port of the Chola kingdom. The city's real name was Kaveripattinam because it was built on the northern banks of the river Kaveri. But poets sometimes called it Kaveripuumpattinam, while the townsfolk called it more affectionately, Puhar, the harbour.

Puhar was actually built in two parts — the port or Maruvurpakkam with its warehouses, its Yavana mansions and traders' streets; and the town itself, Pattinapakkam, whose magnificent centre was the King's palace. Karikala was not only a monarch to be feared by his neighbours, the Pandyas and the Cheras, he had friends in the north, the Kings of Vajra, Magadha and Avanti who wished to be on good terms with him. The palace was full of tributes and gifts from all these places, elaborately displayed. The town had, besides, separate streets for the merchants, Brahmans, astrologers and all the retinue and hangers-on of the palace. To the west, Puhar was fortified, to the east was the open sea; between the town and the port was an open ground planted with trees, where the great daily market was held.

The city had its legends and guardian spirits too. There was a demon who was said to protect the goods left in the warehouses and who would strike blind anyone who dared to meddle with its merchandise. There was the demon at the crossroads, a *bhutam* who devoured false witnesses, dissimulators, villains disguised as holy men and so on. And there was a famous statue of a beautiful girl, placed in an open square, which was said to shed tears — though it never spoke a word in open reproach — if ever a reigning monarch was guilty of the slightest injustice.

As the most important trading centre of the entire Tamil coast, Puhar was a meeting place of many nations and peoples. Caravans from inland places brought their goods for export there — bright gems and gold from Magadha across the Ganga, sweet-smelling sandalwood and spices from the Chera country, the fruit and grain of the Kaveri plains, fine cotton textiles from the south. Meanwhile pearls and branching coral came into Puhar by sea from Korkai and Lanka, and the Yavanas brought their wares from as far away as Egypt and Greece, in big ships carefully guarded against pirates.

Many noble and wealthy men lived in this busy city, among them the two merchant princes Masattuvan and Manaykan who were meeting to discuss the wedding between Kovalan and Kannagi.

Masattuvan came of a proud line of sea-farers. He was foremost among the pearl merchants of the city and had many influential friends in distant Madurai and Korkai in the Pandya country. The King himself acknowledged that he was one of the most important men of Puhar, second only to the royal family. His son Kovalan was sixteen, a dark-skinned, finely-featured elegant youth. He was an accomplished young man too, adept both at singing and at playing the *yaal*, a hand-held harp, of which there were five types, depending on the number of strings. He was popular among the merchant community for he bore himself proudly and spoke well, but some said he had a better talent for music than a head for market prices.

Manaykan was a gentle and generous man. His reputation was such that people compared his kindness to the rain-bearing clouds which appear after a long and parched summer. His was inland trade, he dealt in grain and spices; and the trade route he used lay between Vanji in the Chera country and Puhar. Manaykan's daughter Kannagi was not much more than twelve, for marriages were arranged early in those days. She was a girl with a skin like beaten gold and large clear eyes that seemed to fill her small face. A quiet girl with a rare self-possession.

The two families lived not far from each other in the main street of the merchants and had known each other for many years. The girl and boy had almost grown up together. Recently their parents had noticed how Kovalan's eyes would light up when Kannagi came into the room, or when he saw her, flowers and lamp in hand, as she went with her mother to the temple. It seemed inevitable to the two merchants that their children should marry. In every way it was a suitable and fitting match. They were there that morning mainly to consult the astrologers who would appoint the auspicious day for the wedding, and to conclude the arrangements.

In due course, the astrologer suggested the day when the moon was closest to Rohini, star of happiness. The two fathers agreed and began their preparations in earnest, for the wedding of their only children would be one of Puhar's grand spectacles.

For many years, Kannagi's mother had been collecting her daughter's wedding clothes. She now made a trip to Vanji, the Chera capital, where a jeweller she knew, an old master craftsman, made the girl some fine pieces of jewellery. These included a handsome pair of anklets. Kannagi's mother regretted that they were a bit heavy for the child but it was clear that they would be the pride of her collection.

Days before the wedding, groups of girls, relatives of the two families, were sent throughout the city, mounted on elephants, to announce the wedding and to invite the guests to the bridal feast. On the day itself, so many guests came that it seemed as if the streets leading to Manaykan's house were lined with white parasols waving aloft.

There in front of the house a huge pavilion had been erected. The canopy was made of blue silk embroidered with pearls, and it was held up by pillars decorated with gems and entwined with flower garlands. Drums sounded, conches and pipes blew as the young bride and groom entered the pavilion separately, covered with flowers and jewellery. It might have been a royal procession for all the noise and display. The Brahman priest chanted the wedding rites as Kovalan led his wife, who looked as solemn and remote as a small goddess, around the sacred fire. Then, suddenly it was all over. Women crowded around them, bearing lighted lamps and trays of incense, sandalwood and flowers. They scattered the young couple with flower petals and blessed them, chanting and singing:

May you never be parted
May your love last for ever
May your love be perfect.

The songs of the women were still ringing in Kovalan's ears as he brought his young wife home. They lived, to start with, in Kovalan's parents' house, a vast and luxuriously appointed mansion in which the middle-storey had been set apart for their use.

Kovalan was enchanted by Kannagi's constant presence in his house, and by her beauty and charm which he thought he had never realised sufficiently before. Every day he brought her pretty things as to a playmate — a Yavana lamp may be, a string of flowers, a piece of jewellery that had caught his fancy while walking along the port.

He teased her constantly too, partly because she was solemn by nature and he liked to see the colour rise to her cheeks as she defended herself. 'What do you do with yourself all day,' he asked her, 'while I am learning an honest trade with my father? Just giving your maids endless work, washing and scenting your hair and laying out your jewellery ! In any case, you are so slender that all this jewellery must be terribly heavy for you. It's all vanity, mere vanity!' This, although he knew that she was the least vain of girls, and that she spent most of her day learning about the household from his mother, a strict if kind mentor.

The mansion had wide terraces built on to each storey, meant for the members of the household to sit in quiet and enjoy the moonlight and the cool southern breeze after the heat of the day. But Kovalan noisily chased Kannagi along the carved wooden balconies, and catching her, sometimes painted pictures on her shoulders with sandalwood paste — a clump of sugarcane, a bunch of drooping flowers. This particularly annoyed the girl as she was not at all given to playing romantic games. He always repented, however, when he saw that she was near to tears, and called her fair names, telling her that she was the brightest gem ever mined from the western mountains, sweeter than the legendary nectar distilled from the milk-ocean, rarer than any melody played upon the lute. The peacock and the swan, he told, envied her grace and movement, and the parrot her pretty speech. He meant what he said, but she only begged him not to be so extravagant.

6

Hearing her son's laughter ringing through the house, or his voice raised in argument, Kovalan's mother shook her head and said, 'He will never grow up.' But Masattuvan only replied gently, 'Let us enjoy them while we may, they will be going to their own house soon enough.'

The day eventually came, three years later, when Kovalan and Kannagi were to move into the house which Masattuvan and his wife had built for them. The new house was in many ways a replica of the old one, built three storeys high with balconies and terraces

facing the street. The older woman had herself seen to it that it was appointed with care, with carved bedsteads, painted walls and hangings, and polished silver vessels. Masattuvan had set aside sufficient wealth for the young people to manage their separate household in the customary tradition. And a retinue of attendants, hand-picked and trained with care, were to go with them.

Kannagi stood outside the doors of her new house and drew a sharp breath of delight. They were heavy doors, made of carved teak panels, each with a lotus border. In the centre of each, standing out from an intricate background of flowers and leaves, were a yak, a swan and a goat in strange partnership. She never forgot their presence, after that, every time she went in and out of the house.

The doors opened and they went in together. She seemed at that instant to come into her own, taking up with ease and dignity her position as a young wife and hostess of rank. She knew that both Kovalan's parents and her own looked to her to maintain the traditions and honour of her family. So she began a busy life, observing feast days and fast days, receiving friends and relatives, giving alms to the poor and feeding wandering mendicants. But Kovalan, watching her, sometimes wondered at the speed with which she had outgrown her childhood.

8

2

Madhavi,
the Dancer

Some years after Kovalan and Kannagi were married, in the street of dancers in Puhar a young girl, Madhavi, was getting ready for her first public dance performance.

Madhavi came from no ordinary family. Her mother Chitrapati had always reminded her of this. If ever she complained about the constant music practice, Chitrapati told her once again that their family was descended from the celestial Urvashi herself. And Urvashi, everyone knew, had danced in the courts of the gods.

Chitrapati, a heavy and handsome woman in her thirties, no longer appeared publicly on the stage. All her hopes and ambitions were centred around her young daughter. From the early age of five, for seven years, Madhavi had been put through a course of rigorous training. Every single day her teachers would arrive, the best that Puhar could provide. Morning and evening she sang scales and practised dance movements. More masters came. She learnt to accompany herself on the *yaal*. She learnt the fine points of the flute and drum. Later still came the composers, insisting that she should bring out all possible shades of meaning from every song she sang or danced to.

Chitrapati herself undertook the other aspects of her daughter's education, carefully tutoring her in how to dress and conduct herself. She expected Madhavi to converse intelligently and knowledgeably, but also with wit. Sometimes she made her write poetry to set themes.

Madhavi worked hard, but she seemed to have endless energy. She learnt quickly and well, but then she started with a natural gift for dancing and a quick-witted intelligence. Above all, she was growing strikingly beautiful, with perfect features which were lit with vivacity and laughter. Now, at twelve, she was an accomplished dancer and a carefully finished young lady. Chitrapati at last conceded that Madhavi was ready to start on her own career.

The performance before the King would be a strenuous test, for Puhar was famous not only for its wealth and commerce but also for its fine arts. King Karikala took a great pride in his own court, its brilliant pageantry and ritual, and was known to be a patron of young artists, provided they were truly promising.

As usual an auspicious day was chosen and an auspicious site found. In fact all the details of the wooden stage were established by custom — its length and height, the way the canopy and curtains ought to hang, the correct placing of the guardian deities. There were astrologers and sooth-sayers always at hand, eager to offer advice. But as the construction work went on, Chitrapati, wanting her daughter to be seen to her best advantage, argued endlessly over each stage of the arrangements.

They were hectic days for Chitrapati. But Madhavi went about, unusually tense and quiet, as if in a dream. Nobody consulted her and she was glad to have all the decisions taken out of her hands.

The day arrived; it was nearly time. It was growing dark. A huge oil lamp was lit in front of and a little below the stage. Other lamps had been placed so skilfully that the stage was instantly and brilliantly lit up, there would be no unwanted shadows. Madhavi was waiting now behind the right entrance, beautifully dressed and bejewelled, as still as a statue of Urvashi. No one would have guessed how nervous she was.

At last the royal procession came in — first the royal emblem, the sacred rod which was carried to the centre of the stage by the royal poet; then the King and the minsters who sat themselves in the foremost seats. The blare of conch and drum died down. There was a tense silence.

Madhavi glanced briefly at the older dancers standing a little behind her, then at the singers and musicians who were tuning up, ready to begin. Firmly she entered the stage, right foot first, as she had been taught. There was the faintest tremor in her voice as she sang her songs of invocation of the gods. Then she began to dance, forgetting her mother, the audience, the King; everything except the music and the dance.

Later they said it was a faultless performance. Madhavi was surely the most promising of Puhar's dancers; surely she must rise to fame. They compared the litheness of her movements to a proud, golden creeper. There was a tremendous ovation when the King rose to present her with a green wreath and the customary award of one thousand and eight gold coins.

The royal party left. Madhavi knew that in some strange and subtle way her life had changed. She was on her own from now on; no longer the daughter and pupil for whom every choice was made by others. Turning to her hunchbacked maid, Kuni, she said, 'Take this wreath to the main street where the noblemen of Puhar walk about and say that he who buys it for a thousand gold *kalanjus* may claim Madhavi.'

She looked perfectly calm, eyes wide and gentle as a deer's, her words clear and unhesitating as they reached the last of the guests.

Kovalan who usually attended all the main music and dance performances of Puhar, had been to this one too. He was a discriminating critic, but he had never before been so arrested by the dancer herself. Later he could never explain—not even to himself—the sudden impulse with which he went to the main street and bought the wreath. With a sickening lurch of the heart he followed Kuni to what was now Madhavi's, not Chitrapati's house. Even then he was not sure what to expect. But when he came face to face with Madhavi, it was as if he was bewitched by her vivid beauty and wit. It was as if Kannagi and his home, their quiet life together and all that it stood for belonged to a different world which he set aside or forgot from that moment.

Kovalan did not return home that day nor for many days to come. At first Kannagi was surprised and bewildered. Then at last she realised with a shock that she and her husband had grown very much apart. Kovalan no longer found her seriousness either charming or intriguing; now he thought her perhaps too inflexible in her ways. He was simply more at ease with someone like Madhavi. At last she gave up hope that life would ever resume the even tenor of her early days of marriage.

She went about her usual duties, of course, but it became more and more difficult to keep up appearances, especially as she no longer felt free to dispense hospitality and charities as she would like. Good works continued to be important and meaningful to her and she was hurt, but she said nothing. The only person with whom she could speak freely was her childhood friend, Devandi.

Some days after Madhavi's first performance, Kovalan's parents heard that their son had deserted his wife, and hastened to his house. Kannagi received them alone. At their coming she hurried to put the red auspicious *kumkum* mark on her forehead which she had forgotten that morning, but her mother-in-law noticed immediately

12

that she wore no flowers or jewellery. Kannagi however showed no other outward signs of her sorrow. She greeted them as usual, bringing them fruit and milk and asking after their health.

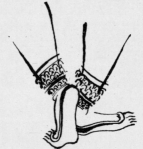

All the same, it turned out to be a difficult situation for both. They, on their part, felt keenly the blow to their family pride; they guessed that Kannagi was alone and unhappy and would have liked to console her, but could not break through her reserve. She on her part found it difficult to accept the sympathy they wanted to give, without in some way seeming disloyal to Kovalan. In the end, Masattuvan and his wife rose to go, saying simply, 'You are always so patient and cheerful, child.' But they left, feeling helpless, and she watched them go with a heavy heart.

It was true that Kovalan had changed in many ways. He stayed at Madhavi's house more and more, coming home only occasionally. Madhavi's house, re-arranged now to suit her own tastes, was full of beautiful objects and rare musical instruments. She practised her music and dancing even more enthusiastically than before and spoke with confidence of these things. Gradually too, her house became a lively centre where interesting people met and conversed — artists, musicians, poets. Kovalan was amazed at Madhavi's great gift for enjoying everything she did. Her description of people and events kept him, as it did all her guests, endlessly entertained.

Madhavi might have been his real wife. When they had a daughter, it seemed to him that it was this child who carried with her,

his destiny and his name. Soon after the child's birth he came upon Chitrapati and her friends playing with the baby. They were discussing names for her, names of famous dancers. He interrupted them sharply. 'I should like the baby to be named after the goddess of my clan, the Goddess of the Sea, Manimekalai,' he said, 'I remember a story my father once told me about one of my ancestors whose ship was caught in a terrible storm and splintered to pieces in the middle of the night. Yet she guided him safely ashore, for she did not forget that he had been a generous man. She has always been our guardian.'

Madhavi was delighted by the name, and so it was decided. They celebrated the naming day in lavish style. Madhavi was radiantly happy as she sat next to Kovalan and received the hundreds of friends and relatives who came to bless the child. On that occasion, Kovalan gave away handfuls of gold to the Brahmans who assisted in the rites.

Kovalan changed in other ways too, becoming almost recklessly generous. The daily acts of charity that Kannagi believed in were not his style. He was more impulsive, but more flamboyant as well. Strangely, in those days, he felt most compassionate towards people who had somehow fallen into error.

At one time he heard of a Brahman woman who had killed a mongoose by mistake. She had intended to strike out at the snake it was fighting with, but her aim was poor. Troubled by what she had done, she ran to her husband, for the scriptures said that to kill a mongoose was a very sinful act. The Brahman was a cold and orthodox man who stuck to the letter of the law. To his wife's horror, he said he would have nothing more to do with her. He then planned to leave home on a long pilgrimage. Frantically she pleaded with him to help her. He relented so far as to leave her a palm leaf inscription. 'It tells you what you may do to save yourself,' he said, 'But you will need the help of a rich patron. I cannot afford the charities that are prescribed.' He left home immediately after that.

Someone visiting Madhavi's house mentioned the poor woman's plight. Kovalan at once went out and brought the palm leaf inscription and himself performed the charities which would absolve her guilt. He brought back the woman's husband and settled a small part of his wealth upon them so that their future might be secure.

An even stranger incident happened later. It began with someone accusing a perfectly honest woman of being false to her husband. Now the *bhutam* at the crossroads whose duty it was to discover and capture false witnesses did so in this case as well. The woman was cleared of suspicion, and the man who had accused her wrongfully was held in a noose, at the mercy of the *bhutam*. Kovalan, chancing to come that way, found the *bhutam* just about to execute the man, his old mother weeping by his side. Stricken by the old lady's grief, Kovalan at once offered his life in exchange for the culprit's. Of course this could not be; the *bhutam* refused the offer and so the culprit died. But Kovalan accompanied the old lady home and did indeed take the place of her son, looking after her for many years and keeping her from want.

15

A few years passed by. Madhavi continued to be radiantly happy, both in her private life with Kovalan and her growing daughter, and also in her public performances. Her dance was improving all the time, her fame had begun to spread throughout the Chola country. The finest of musicians now considered it an honour to accompany her.

But things gradually altered for Kovalan. In the first place he was spending far too much on wild acts of generosity and lavish presents to Madhavi and Manimekalai. At last he began to realise that the large part of his ancestral property which had been set aside for him was slowly dwindling away. He could not ask his father and so he began to sell his own and Kannagi's possessions, much though he hated himself for doing so. He also began to feel that he was no longer in his first youth, and that he had wasted his years away. A kind of disaffection seemed to creep into his life, poisoning his pleasure in everything. Even his luxurious life with Madhavi began to feel irksome, as if he were trapped.

The years had drifted on, the child Manimekalai was nearly eight. It was time for the Indra festival once more. Splendid as Puhar was right through the year, the city was at its finest every summer when a festival in honour of Indra, King of the gods, was held there. This festival had been founded by an ancient King, Thodi-thod-chempiyan, and every succeeding Chola King had kept up the tradition.

Days before, all the streets were swept and sanded, then decorated with flower garlands and flags. Lamps and golden vases filled with water were placed in front of all the shops and houses. Many of the great mansions put out specially decorated stands in their balconies and let down brilliantly coloured streamers and banners over their doorways.

On the first day of the festival, the royal procession left the palace, led by the King himself. He was followed by the chief ministers of state, the five great assemblies, the eight groups of attendants and then the nobility of the city all according to rank and order, mounted on chariots and splendidly caparisoned elephants and horses. The procession slowly made its way through crowded and cheering streets to the banks of the river Kaveri. Here the young men of the royal family filled golden pots with the sacred waters. Slowly the procession returned to the great temple, this time with the young men in the lead, burnished pots on their heads glinting in the early morning sun. The god was bathed in the river waters while music played, drums sounded and people cheered and sang.

These were only the opening rites of the Indra festival; for worship was held and various other rituals performed in all the temples of Puhar during the following days. The festivities went on for twenty-eight days, with dance performances, song and story recitals, market fairs and all sorts of other side-shows.

It was the last day of the festival. Madhavi had played a prominent part in the festivities that year. She had fulfilled the promise of her early years and was now at the very peak of her career. Her performances were crowded with people from all over the Tamil country and even from far northern states who had come to Puhar for the festival and in particular to see her dance.

That year she had danced in an elaborate series of eleven dances of the gods, beginning with Shiva's dance of destruction, and ending with Indrani's dance at the northern gates of the city of Vana. She had been absorbed in this for days, rehearsing strenuously and planning out every detail. The audience had received her enthusiastically, and she returned home from the last of the series, tired but triumphant.

16

She found Kovalan seated alone, in a strange and saddened mood. He had hardly taken part in the merry-making, preferring to be alone. But that morning, by chance, he had joined a small group of people gathered around a Jain holy woman and ascetic who was preaching the value of a life of restraint and discipline. Something

about her, her voice perhaps, or that look of absolute renunciation had made a deep impression on him. And what she said agreed with his own mood, his gathering sense of wasted years.

But Madhavi did not know this. She herself was aware of a sense of disenchantment after all those days of excitement and she thought that Kovalan must feel the same way. She realised with a pang of regret that she had seen very little of him in the past month. She ought to make up for that by lifting him out of his listlessness now.

She made a special effort to make herself beautiful for him. She washed, oiled and scented her hair and arranged it in five elaborate plaits—high fashion in those days. She painted the soles of her feet red and slipped rings on each little toe. On her feet she wore an ornament held at the ankle and the big toe, and made up of a fine mesh of gold chains strung with pearls. For each ankle she chose four anklets, one of which was made of tiny golden bells and another of intricately plaited gold wire. She then selected a length of fine blue silk, draped it around her waist, and held it in place with a girdle made of thirty-two strands of perfect pearls. Armlets, then, clasping her firm upper arm, and a profusion of bangles and bracelets from elbow to finely-turned wrist. She chose a set of

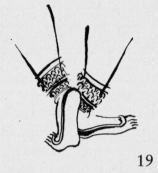

necklaces and chains to wear round her neck, arranging them so that each showed to its best effect. Finally she slipped on a pair of splendid sparkling earrings. At last she was ready, looking more beautiful than she had ever done before.

She begged Kovalan prettily that they should go and join in the last of the merry-making—the princes and the nobles went to bathe and sport in the river on the last day of the Indra festival, could they not go too? He could not resist her plea; he agreed.

It was late at night when they crossed the main street, she in her chariot, he on horseback alongside, making their way towards the beach. The ships lay quietly in the harbour, huge shadowy shapes, but there were lights everywhere else. The brilliant beacon of the lighthouse shone far out to sea, while there, in the distant horizon, were tiny twinkling lights from the fishing boats. On the shore were the lights of the tradesmen who were still trying to strike a last bargain, the torches of the night watchmen, lamps from little stalls selling flowers and snacks. The merry-makers were still in groups all along the beach, some indeed still splashing and bathing in the water when they arrived. Quickly her maids set up a little enclosure with painted canvas screens under a flowering tree which Madhavi pointed out.

She led Kovalan there. The sea sounded close by, but its acrid smell was obliterated by the scent of the flowers. Madhavi always thought of every comfort. She now took her favourite *yaal* from the hands of her maid, Vasantamalai, she lifted off its embroidered casing, tuned it, strummed upon it for a while, and then turned to Kovalan with a charming smile. 'What would you like to sing?'

At first he seemed completely won over. He took the harp from her hands, he seemed happy; without hesitation he began a song in praise of the river Kaveri.

> Long may you live, Kaveri !
> And may you never grieve, even if our garlanded King
> Who carries the white umbrella of compassion
> Who spreads the reign of justice
> Should fall in love with the Ganga.
> As the best of wives, you will forgive him, we know.
> So long may you live, Kaveri.

He followed this up with a song praising Puhar. But after that his mood seemed to change; he began a series of love songs set among the fisherfolk, *kanal-vari* or sea-shore lyrics. All of them were sad songs of parting and loss.

> Sweet smelling garden flowers, blowing over fresh sea sand,
> Your perfect words spoken there,
> Your young breasts, the bright moon of your face,
> Your arched eyebrows like twin bows,
> Oh, your impossibly tiny waist
> — How they have shaken my heart.

> A shoreline lapped with waves, clean sands spreading,
> Drifting flower scents from the garden,
> The smell of your long hair, your face pure as the moon,
> Oh, the look from your wide carp-shaped eyes,
> — How they tug at my heart.

20

> A beach covered with shells, and a garden heady with scent,
> Flowers just beginning to shed their petals,
> Those secret places which are yours alone,
> Your smile, like a string of buds,
> Oh, your moon face and your tender breasts
> — How they fill me with pain.

He ended with a short and bitter lyric:

Foolish swan, do not draw near her,
You cannot compete with her grace.
She will walk the whole wide earth
Even to its shimmering watery edges
Betraying men.
Do not follow her, foolish swan,
For your innocent ways are not hers.

There was a sharpness of tone, a peculiar resonance to these songs which cut Madhavi to the heart. Could it be that he intended a reference to her? If so, why should he? However, she was much too self-controlled to show any offence. She never openly quarrelled; her training had after all provided her with the means to deal tactfully with all awkward situations. So now her wide eyes betrayed nothing of her distress as she took the harp from Kovalan and sang to him as if in answer, song for song.

She too began with songs in praise of the Kaveri and of Puhar, then she sang the love songs of the fisherfolk. But her theme was that of a lonely and forsaken fisher-girl lamenting for her absent lover. She wanted to assure Kovalan that she would keep faith with him whatever he might choose to think.

She sang:

Bird-song is quiet now, the day's King has vanished now,
Endless tears hurt my tired eyes.
Tell me, my friend, you who wear the jasmine buds in your hair,
Does this darkening sky come to torment me
From that far country where he is gone?

Now Kovalan had a fine voice, certainly, but Madhavi sang with such piercing sweetness, wringing such pathos out of her songs that Kovalan was disturbed in his turn. And by a strange quirk of fate, the effect of her singing was exactly the opposite of what she intended.

'I only sang songs to amuse her,' he said to himself. 'But what is she after? It is clear she has lost her heart to someone else and is trying to conceal her deceit.'

Aloud he said brusquely, 'It is far too late, I must go,' and he left immediately, without further word.

Madhavi was too stunned to think of anything but his discourtesy. For a while she sat there alone, looking out at the distant and dark sea. The breeze blew cold. She shivered. She called her attendants, climbed into her carriage and left for home.

21

Madhavi had arranged for herself a little summer room at the top of her house, sheltered, yet airy and cool and full of flowers. Here she made her way alone the next day, to think about what she should do. After that disastrous evening she had grown very alarmed by Kovalan's attitude. She was now in anguish to think that he was drifting away from her. She loved him deeply and could not imagine a life apart from him, after all these years together. She would have to use all her wits and charm to win him back as tactfully as she could. But what could she do?

For some time she played to herself on her *yaal*, but it only deepened her grief. Suddenly she put it aside and came to a decision. She gathered together a number of flowers — champak, jasmine and others, interspersed with green leaves and sweet-smelling roots. Skilfully she made a garland, subtly, evocatively scented; red flowers alternating with white. When it was done, she selected a single perfectly-formed white flower and inscribed a message on it with red writing-paste:

> Early summer is prince-regent now, forcing all
> Living creatures to thoughts of love.
> The unkind moon, appearing above the troubled sunset
> Frowns on parted lovers.
> And the God of Love does not fail to torment
> The lonely.
> I think you will understand.

By the time she had finished writing the message, she had regained her spirits; she was actually humming to herself. She had not made a scene, she had not heaped recriminations on his head, she had managed it with the utmost skill. She had not been trained in the sixty-four arts so early and for so long in vain. Surely he would not resist her appeal. Surely he must come. She clapped her hands and summoned Vasantamalai.

'Take this to Kovalan,' she said to her. 'Put this garland in his hands and repeat to him the message I have written here. I trust you to find him and bring him to me, Vasantamalai!'

Vasantamalai ran all the way along the market street looking for Kovalan and found him at last. He was sitting with some merchants, trying to balance his accounts. She called him aside and held out the garland, repeating the message.

Unfortunately it was Madhavi's worst mistake. To Kovalan in his present mood, it struck exactly the wrong jarring note. He looked at the garland — it seemed so contrived and yet so blatant with its alternate red and white. And the message! So ornate, with its summer prince-regent and God of Love and unkind moon. Just like her, all artifice, artifice! He was finished with hidden meanings and exquisite games.

'I have seen your mistress in every kind of role,' he said to Vasantamalai. 'Yes, she gives quite a convincing performance. But you see, I know by now that it is all a game to her. She is after all an actress.'

He turned away in open hostility and returned to his calculations, only to find that his capital had come to an end at last.

Vasantamalai could do nothing more. She looked down at the garland which she still held in her hands and knew that Madhavi had woven it with as much love as with skill — that was the way Madhavi was. He had not even touched it. She went home quietly and told her mistress all that had happened.

Madhavi listened. She would not believe that Kovalan had left her forever. 'Well,' she said, putting a brave face on it, 'if he won't come this evening, we may surely expect him tomorrow morning.'

But in her heart she was full of grief.

3
The Journey

It was the evening of the same day, a time when the young married women of Puhar were scattering the floors of their houses with auspicious jasmine buds and rice grains, and lighting their lamps in order to welcome home their husbands. Kannagi alone sat by herself without hope. This evening she was even more depressed than usual.

Her friend, Devandi, who knew that Kannagi tended to be particularly sad in the evenings, came to visit her. She had just been to the temple to make offerings and to pray to the gods to intercede on her friend's behalf. She entered the house now and blessed Kannagi, saying, 'You too will soon welcome your husband.'

'O Devandi,' said Kannagi, 'I thank you for your kind words, but in my heart I doubt whether it can ever be. I'm so afraid. I had such a strange dream last night; my husband and I were walking hand in hand towards a vast and glorious city. I was happy, everything seemed good and right again. But suddenly someone came and accused him of a terrible thing. Do you know that even in my dream I felt a sharp scorching pain, as if... as if I were stung by a scorpion. Then I was running wildly to protest before the King. Can you imagine me doing that ! After that it all became very violent and confused... I can't remember anything more.'

She was quiet for some time. Then she said, 'Perhaps it was only a nightmare. Perhaps you'll remember this and laugh one day when Kovalan and I are happy together again. When will that be? In heaven?'

Devandi was distressed. She said softly, 'Kannagi don't be sad. Listen to me now. Your husband hasn't rejected you, he doesn't hate you. What you suffer now may well be because you failed to fulfil a vow which you made in a former life. Listen, you know of the two ponds sacred to the sun and the moon outside the city walls, just where the Kaveri meets the sea. I have heard it said that women who bathe there and then worship the God of Love live happily married lives throughout this birth and for ever afterwards. Come Kannagi, let us go there one day.'

Kannagi began, 'It would not be proper for me to do that —

It was at this very moment that an attendant, a retainer of the family for many years who had known Kannagi since she was a young girl, came running in.

'The master is coming home,' she cried, 'My lady, my lady, the guardian of this house is returning!' Hearing this, Devandi smiled and left at once.

Husband and wife were face to face at last, after many years. He saw how frail she looked, standing before him, even plain, bereft of all ornaments and decoration. At one time he had chided her maids for overloading her with ornaments. They did nothing, he used to say, to enhance her natural beauty, and anyway she was too slightly built to bear the weight of all those gems and gold. Where were all those jewels now? He himself had sold most of them when he needed money. He was overcome with shame and regret.

'All these years I've lived with a woman who cannot tell the difference between truth and falsehood. On such a woman I have wasted all my ancestral wealth. I bring you nothing but poverty. I'm bitterly ashamed.'

But she smiled a radiant and serene smile as if she were coming out of her nightmare at last.

'There are still my gold anklets,' she said simply, 'Take them.'

She gave him a small ray of hope. He hesitated a moment and then spoke, 'Kannagi, perhaps it is possible. Perhaps I could use these as capital and set up a business which will slowly grow and regain all that I have lost through my folly. I could do it. But not here. I cannot bear to live in Puhar anymore.'

It was true. It came to him with sudden certainty that he must make a clean break with his past; it must be complete and absolute.

'Will you go with me?' he asked her. 'Let's go right away, far south to Madurai in the heart of the Pandya kingdom. Madurai will have many opportunities for me. We could start a new life together, you and I. Come Kannagi, let us go this very night, before daybreak.

Kovalan was determined to leave that very night. He did not even wish to let his parents know, for they might deter him from his purpose. Nor must the attendants know. They would walk all the way and they did not wish to be burdened, so they took no possessions with them except the anklets.

Long before the first light broke, they softly stole downstairs, drew the bolt of the gate quietly and stepped outside. Kovalan pushed the great heavy doors together and closed them. From their ornate carved surface the strange animals and birds seemed to stare

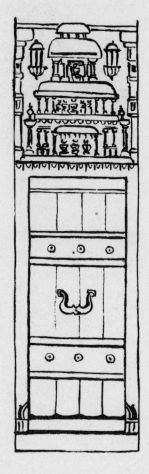

dispassionately into the dim light. Kannagi touched the swan, the goat and the yak in a quiet gesture of farewell, remembering the affectionate care with which Kovalan's parents had built them this house.

The streets were dark and quiet and empty. They passed the great Vishnu temple and seven Buddhist *viharas* said to have been built by the god Indra himself. Then they came to a pedestal of polished black stone where wandering Jain monks came and preached on festival days. Not far from here Kovalan had heard the holy woman speak about the path to spiritual liberation. Now they walked round the stone in salutation to the ascetic men and women, and then took the broad road beyond it, leading to the city gates.

At last they came out of the high winding walls. The royal parks and lakes lay before them, and beyond that a moat which could be crossed by a small parapet. There, beyond the moat, lay the road westward which would take them to Madurai! The early morning light was just breaking, colouring sky and water a pale gold. Kovalan's heart lifted.

'Out of Puhar at last, my love,' he said.

Kannagi looked back at the trees in the parks, full of early summer flowers, and the great walls which now hid the city from her view. Yes, Puhar was beautiful, but she too had had enough of it.

They now took the avenue westwards, along the north bank of the Kaveri for about ten miles or a *kavatham*. The sun was beginning to climb high in the sky when they reached a dense grove. It was a well-known spot, because a recluse, a Jain holy woman, had her hermitage there.

Kannagi sat down under a shady tree. She had never left Puhar before, neither had she walked this far. Her feet hurt, although she would not admit it.

'Is it much further to Madurai?' she asked.

26

'No, not much.' He was in good spirits now, but touched by her innocence. 'Only thirty *kavathams* out of which we have walked one! Come, you must rest a little now. Let us go into the hermitage and pay our respects to the renunciant, Kavundi, if she is there.'

'I have heard of her, she is famous for her penances and austerities,' said Kannagi, with some trepidation.

They went a little further, and came to a clump of rocks surrounding what looked like a natural cave. Above the narrow entrance was a make-shift projection of leaves and thatch which would keep out the rain. Inside it was bare and quiet; there was a rough ledge in the rock where she probably slept. That was all. The *sadhvi* was there, gaunt and tall, even when sitting cross-legged. She was old, draped in a cloth once white, now grey, shaven head covered. Even her face seemed grey. Kovalan instantly recognised her. The preaching sadhvi! It seemed inevitable that they should meet. They prostrated themselves before her and she blessed them; her hands were gentle and firm. She said in that deep voice that Kovalan remembered,

'From your looks and manners, I can see that you two are well-born. Why then have you left your home? Why are you travelling like this on foot, as if you were a pair of destitutes?'

If she recognised Kovalan, she gave no sign of it and now he met her startlingly clear eyes.

'I wish to go to Madurai to seek my fortune,' he said firmly, 'I can say no more.'

She made no further enquiries into their lives, but her eyes turned to Kannagi's slight form.

'This girl is delicate,' she said, 'Do you know what you are asking her to do? The road to Madurai is long and rough, leading through wilderness and jungle. Yet I can see that I could not dissuade you from this journey, even if I wished to.' Her voice was stern.

For many years, ever since she took her vows, this woman had struggled to free her mind of anger, envy and desire; to live only by the principle of never telling a lie and never harming a living creature. She lived alone for four months of the year at this hermitage, entering the town briefly to preach or to beg an occasional meal. People came out to her, sometimes for spiritual advice, sometimes simply to pay their respects and receive her blessings. The rest of the year she went on long pilgrimages on foot, to holy places or to communities of renunciants where she could hear sermons and explanations of the Jain scriptures. For long she had given up all involvement with the world. But now she was moved by the sight of these two young people who seemed to bear the marks of some unknown suffering. She looked again at Kannagi, who immediately sensed this flow of sympathy.

'Listen,' said Kavundi adigal, 'It is time for me, too, to leave Puhar. For some time past, I too have been contemplating a journey to Madurai, for there are many holy monks there who could teach me much about the Eternal Law. I wish, too, to visit the shrine of Arivan at Uraiyur. Let us go together.'

Kovalan was surprised when she said this, but also relieved. It suddenly came to him that perhaps he had not calculated the dangers and difficulties of this journey. Kavundi's presence would be a great comfort. He said so.

The adigal at once slung her water-pot in its bag of twine on her back and took up her begging bowl. In her right hand she carried a bundle of peacock feathers with which she would gently sweep off insects without injuring them. She prayed briefly and was ready to go.

And so, with Kavundi adigal striding in front, they set off towards Madurai.

It was Kavundi who chose the route they should take, which went along the banks of the Kaveri, passing partly through the fields and partly through the jungle. This was perhaps the best part of the entire journey, full of fresh country sights for these townsfolk.

The Kaveri was the chief reason for the rich fertility of this stretch of land. From distant Kudakam (or Coorg) she took her source and it was said that she flowed through the Chola country at the request of the ancient sage Agastya himself. Certainly here she was at her widest and most forceful. There used to be frequent floods in these parts until King Karikala organised the construction of high banks along the sides, and a series of sluices and canals to carry the river water into the neighbouring fields. Now the travellers could hear the roaring of the water rushing through water-locks and drowning all other sounds.

Sometimes they walked through water-logged forests, thick with lotuses underfoot and encircled by sugarcane fields. Here the air was full of the sounds of natural wild life : the humming of insects, the cries of the wild fowl, the wheeling and shrieking of cranes and storks, wild geese and other water-birds. There were wild water-buffaloes too, ambling past, red-eyed and streaked with mud.

In the fields the peasants, men and women, were hard at work. There were women standing knee-deep in the rice fields transplanting the young rice-shoots. Unadorned as they were and mudstained, they seemed to Kovalan beautiful ; as if they were sprung from the land. Then there were the ploughmen nearby, singing the song of the plough as they walked along the straight, deep furrows. Further off they could hear threshing songs from cowherds as they watched the cattle stamping out the first harvest, separating chaff from grain. Everywhere there were little villages, settlements and shrines; smoke rising high from recent sacrificial

28

offerings. It seemed a land of peace, where people had enough to meet their needs, where they worked hard and yet were merry.

The travellers walked slowly along enjoying all these sights until at last, after many days of travelling, they reached the garden city of Srirangam, in an island made by the river.

The contrast was sudden — here was the town again, with houses and well-made gardens. The subtle scent of the cultivated flowers wafted to them as they walked along a wide street, bringing to Kovalan, at least, disturbing thoughts and memories. He gave himself an impatient shake and noticed that Kavundi and Kannagi had prostrated themselves before an approaching monk. He followed suit.

The Jain monk looked at the strange group in front of him. He knew Kavundi a little, for he too came from Puhar, and it was to her that he addressed himself :

'Hear my words, pious Kavundi! You know that no one ever escaped the effect of his own good or evil deeds. For each of our actions is like a seed that is sown and is bound to bring a harvest of its own kind. Moreover, you know that life is fleeting — our lives leave our bodies as quickly as the flame leaves the lamp when it is set out upon a desert with a wild wind blowing. Remember then, that it is only through the teachings of Arivan, embodiment of the Eternal Law, that we can free ourselves from the endless chains that imprison us within the cycle of rebirth. May you be free from the bonds of desire.'

His blessing included all three, and they echoed his last words, 'May we be freed from all bonds of desire.'

They were all subdued after this encounter, each absorbed in their own thoughts. They came out of Srirangam and took the ferry across to the south bank from where they would walk towards Uraiyur, the old Chola capital. By the time they crossed over, though, Kavundi could see that the young couple were tired, even dispirited. She was more determined than ever not to pry into their affairs; she simply suggested that they might rest for a while in a flowery grove near a temple.

Kavundi sat under a shady tree to meditate and closed her eyes. Kovalan and Kannagi moved a little further off to a grassy bank where Kannagi lay down, resting her head on Kovalan's lap. He noticed the lines on her forehead and gently smoothed them out. All was quiet. Suddenly they heard shrieks of laughter and a young man

30

burst into the grove followed by a girl. The man walked with a swagger, intending to show off, while the girl made silly jokes. They appeared to be a thoughtless pair.

'Oh, there is someone here ahead of us.'

'Look at this — Kama, the God of Love himself, and Rati, his wife!'

'I wonder who they are. Shall I ask the old lady?'

'You wouldn't dare?'

But of course he would. He swaggered up to Kavundi and began with exaggerated deference.

'Revered sage, who are this couple who have attached themselves to you?'

Kavundi opened her eyes and gave the young man a piercing look. Her voice was sharp when she spoke.

'These are my children. They are ordinary human beings. Leave them alone. Can't you see they are tired?'

They did not hear the warning note in her voice. The girl sniggered; this set the boy off.

'Your children? O, most holy ascetic! Do tell me, you who must be so learned, can Kama and Rati be brother and sister ?'

Kannagi, who heard this remark, stood up trembling and put her hands over her ears. Kavundi adigal's eyes flashed, her voice was like a whiplash as she cursed them.

'Thoughtless ones! You are no more than jackals who belong to the thorny jungle.'

No sooner had she spoken than the curse took effect. The youth and the girl disappeared. Something scurried past. They could hear the jackals howling weirdly in the distance.

Kovalan and Kannagi were really shaken now. How one rash blunder may alter the entire course of one's life, thought Kovalan. And quickly he said,

'They shouldn't have spoken to you as they did, it's true. But dear saint, they are very young and didn't realise what they were doing.' Gently, Kannagi added, 'Tell us how soon you may release them from this curse.'

'Disrespect is no small thing, Kovalan,' said Kavundi 'nor is thoughtlessness. Yet it was for Kannagi's sake that I chiefly minded. Perhaps, as you two seem to think, I was too harsh. Well, let these two live in the jungle surrounding the fortress walls for twelve months. After that they may regain their original form.'

They left the grove still heavy-hearted, and walked away, past the ancient fortifications, to Uraiyur itself. There was an ancient Jain shrine in this city, adjacent to a monastery, and they made their way there. They found the image of Arivan, the Perfected One, seated in the lotus position under an Asoka tree. The triple umbrella above his head looked like three moons, stacked one above the other. His face looked down upon them serenely, speaking somehow of simplicity and peace. Kavundi knelt at his feet for some time ; then she took the two young people into the monastery with her, and there they rested for the whole day.

But Kovalan was anxious now to turn southwards, to Madurai. They were now leaving the Chola country, however, and would need advice about the roads to take. Fortunately, a Brahman pilgrim came that way and asked them who they were and which way they were going.

'We wish to go to Madurai,' said Kovalan. 'Can you tell us the quickest way?'

'Oh, that's by no means an easy question to answer,' said the Brahman, a cheerful and loquacious man. 'But first of all, what a pity you're travelling in this season! It's high summer now, all the land is parched and dry, even the paths have all worn away, leaving only the sharp stones exposed. The young lady is going to have a terrible time! But then, you have Madurai to look forward to. O, Madurai is splendid. And you've heard of the great King Nedunchezhiyan.'

'But I must answer your question. First of all, you must take the road to the lake at Kodumbai, and it's a rough road, I warn you. From there, you have three possibilities. On the right, there is a jungle track, passing through a country inhabited by wild hunting

tribes. That way you'll get to the Sirumalai hills, beyond which, on the left lies Madurai.'

'Now the route to the left from Kodumbai is an interesting one too, for it passes by a hill where there is an underground passage leading to three miraculous lakes. If you bathe in these, one will give you divine knowledge, the second will give you knowledge of past deeds, and the third will fulfil your slightest wish. There is a valley nearby too, guarded by a goddess who is wont to torment you with riddles. But if you answer her well, she too will lead you to these lakes.

'Of course, there is the middle path passing through villages and groves. It is a bit thorny and overgrown but it is safe.'

'Sir,' said Kavundi, 'we thank you. We have no need of miraculous lakes and helpful celestial beings. It is our present deeds alone that reveal past ones; it is only by seeking truth and kindness that we fulfil our lives. Go in peace: we'll follow our own paths.

They turned their steps southwards. The pilgrim had been right, it was much hotter now and the road lay through jungle. From now on the journey would no longer be pleasant. Kavundi could go for many days without food and with very little water, but she was concerned for Kannagi.

One day, soon after they left Uraiyur, Kovalan left Kannagi and Kavundi resting by the main road and followed a side-path in search of water. Here at last he came to a little pond and bent down to slake his thirst. A rustle behind him made him turn round. To his horror and surprise he saw Vasantamalai, Madhavi's maid, running towards him. The next moment she fell at his feet. She was trembling, her large upturned eyes were swimming with tears.

'My lord, Madhavi turned me away when I returned to her with your message,' she said, as if it was but yesterday that he had refused the garland. 'My mistress wept saying, "There was nothing wrong in the message I wrote on the wreath. How could there be? I cannot understand why Kovalan should be so cruel to me, unless you told him some lie." Poor woman, she was beside herself with grief. She cursed her life which seemed somehow to turn away good and pious people. Then with a sudden frantic gesture she tore at her necklace, scattering pearls everywhere, and in her bitterness and fury she rounded on me and turned me out... What could I do? I heard that you had left for Madurai, so I joined a group of travellers coming this way. Now that I've found you, please don't desert me.'

Kovalan was sorely troubled. At the back of his mind, the incident of the flower garland still rankled. On that occasion he had been

wilfully, knowingly hurtful. He felt a pang of remorse. Yet would he never be free of Madhavi and her machinations? He looked at the girl in front of him and she suddenly seemed false to him, just as her mistress and her message had seemed false. How, anyway, did Vasantamalai know that he was going to Madurai? As the doubt assailed him, the girl seemed to become unreal, illusory. He stilled his turbulent mind and spoke an invocation to the gods.

It was indeed an illusion, disappearing like a troubled dream, leaving behind only a voice, a whisper, which seemed to say, ' I am only a forest spirit who wished to tempt you. Forgive me. Keep this incident to yourself; do not tell of it to your innocent wife, or even to that saint.'

He took the water he had come to fetch in lotus leaves which he shaped roughly into cups and returned to the women who were still

34

sitting where he had left them. Thank heavens he could still meet the
sadhvi's clear eyes. They drank the water gratefully, but he knew
they could not walk much further in the burning heat. So he led them
to a nearby temple at whose steps they could rest.

It was here that Kannagi gave in to tears for the first and only time
during the journey.

Again their peace was shattered, this time by a fierce-looking
group of people, men and women, emerging from some huts in the
forest. The men were tall and hardy with curly hair and beards; some
were carrying bows and arrows, others were sounding double-
headed drums to a rousing rhythm.

'Who are they?' asked Kannagi, really frightened this time.

'Tribal people, I should think. Hunters, by the look of them. They
are human beings too, child. I think you'll find that they are coming
here to worship. Let them worship in their way, I'll do so in mine.'
And Kavundi retired to some distance.

'They must be Eynar or Vedar,' said Kovalan. He had heard of
these people who lived by stealing cattle and plundering. They were
said to be such fierce fighters that they resisted the Chola army with
ease. Kovalan had never met any of them before and was excited. He
took Kannagi's hand to reassure her.

Kavundi was right, they were coming to the very shrine where
they sat. They hastily stepped aside, noticing now the image inside.
It was the image of Aiyai, goddess of the hunters, a weird and
awesome figure. Her matted hair was gathered in a knot at the top
of her head and tied with snake-skin; a curved boar's tusk,
resembling a crescent moon, was fastened in front. She wore a
necklace made of tigers' teeth, and her only garment was a tiger-skin
draped at her waist. In her hand she carried a bow with which she
was just about to shoot, and she was mounted on a stag with tall,
branching antlers.

As the travellers stepped aside, the women came forward first of
all, to make curious offerings of toys, dolls and then of small game-
birds, some of which they sacrificed. Suddenly a strange thing
happened. A young woman pushed her way through the crowd and
came forward. She was dressed exactly as the goddess in the shrine
was, and was apparently her priestess and representative. All the
drums were sounding now, faster and faster, as the crowd fell back a
little, leaving an open space.

The young woman began to sway slowly, and then to dance,
trembling and shaking. Finally she stopped and spoke in a loud,
hoarse voice:

'The cattle stalls in all our neighbouring villages are full, their herds prosper; but the commonly held lands of the Eynar stand bare and empty. How can this be? Have you Eynar lost your pride and courage? Have you become stupid and apathetic like peace-loving peasants? Come now, rouse yourselves. Make your sacrifices to the goddess who rides upon the stag, otherwise she will not bless you with victory.'

After this, everyone seemed to go wild. The men prepared a buffalo for sacrifice; then there were a number of songs and dances in which the entire village took part. All this while no one had taken any notice of the travellers. Kannagi had lost her initial fear of this tribe, she was almost as fascinated as Kovalan was. She listened as they sang to the goddess:

> The tiger-skin at your waist, the elephant-hide covering you,
> You stand upon the wild buffalo's black head, for all of us to see.
> Yet the gods bow before you, for you are the sacred mystery,
> The secret flame of knowledge.
>
> You stand proudly upon the stag,
> Your braclet-laden hand brandishing the dripping sword
> With which you killed the buffalo demon.
> Yet you are the inward light from the lotus hearts
> Of Vishnu, Shiva and Brahma.
>
> You stand upon an angry, red-eyed lion, the conch and the discus
> In your lotus hands.
> Yet you are also at the side of him who bears the third eye
> And carries the Ganga in his hair;
> You are she whom the Vedas praise.

All of a sudden the young woman who had been possessed by the goddess earlier came out of the circle of dancers and walked towards Kannagi. She raised her finger to point at her and called out in a loud, ringing voice:

'She has come to us, the treasure of the northern Kongu Nadu, the mistress of the western Kuda mountains, Queen of the southern Tamil country, matchless jewel of the whole earth!'

When Kannnagi heard this, she was extremely embarrassed and stepped back a little so that she was hidden by her husband, saying softly, 'She doesn't know what she is saying.'

But Kovalan looked at his wife with shining eyes. She was so quiet, even timid about little things. But underneath it all, there was

such courage and endurance. Perhaps this unkown woman, possessed as she was by the goddess, could sense immediately this quality, which he had taken so long to find.

It was nearly dawn when the Eynar men and women left for their homes and Kovalan and Kannagi went to find Kavundi adigal. When they neared her Kovalan said, 'We are now in the Pandya country and we need have no fear of robbers and theives, for the highways are well-guarded and safe here. I think that even wild beasts are unlikely to trouble us. Would it not be best to travel by night and rest during the day? I am afraid Kannagi can no longer bear the fierce heat.'

Kavundi agreed, and so they rested and waited until the sun had gone down. At last it was time to go. Kovalan smiled at his wife. 'Tonight you may hear the distant hooting of the night-owl and the growling of bears. Perhaps wild animals may even cross our paths. But you won't be afraid, will you?'

In answer, she merely stood up, ready to leave. He took her hand and put it on his shoulder and so they set off once more. Kavundi, instead of striding ahead, walked with them telling them stories from the lives of the saints, until at last the wildfowl in the bamboo thickets called out the coming of the day.

They came to a Brahman village, and here again Kovalan left his wife and the renunciant resting while he went in search of water. He was thinking, as he went along, how easily he had decided to leave Puhar, and how unpredictable and strange this journey was proving to be. He passed a tree under which a young Brahman was resting. The young man looked up and his searching eyes rested on Kovalan for a long moment. Then he turned away, and said aloud, as if addressing a withered creeper,

'How desolate you look in this summer, bare of all flowers. You might be Madhavi herself, alone in her sorrow.'

Kovalan stopped short, dismayed at what he heard.

'Why do you say that? What could you possibly mean?' he asked

The young man jumped to his feet and ran towards him exclaiming, 'At last I have found you. For a moment I wasn't quite sure. I knew you by sight in Puhar, but you look so changed. How thin and brown you look! And dressed so plainly too!' He was, he explained, a priest from Puhar, called Kausikan. 'I bring you news from your home,' he said, 'and also a letter. Your parents are profoundly grieved; it is as if they had lost their brightest treasure. All your relatives are puzzled and unhappy. Your servants have gone

38

off in all directions in order to find you and bring you home. But it was Madhavi who took it the hardest when she heard through Vasantamalai of your disappearance. She was absolutely shocked and quite inconsolable. I went to see her, hearing of her extreme distress. Do you know, she fell at my feet like a suppliant. Madhavi is changed too... all that pride and composure gone. Anyway, she gave me this letter to take to you, saying, 'Give this to him who is dearer than my own eyes.'

Kovalan took the letter silently. The seal over the folded palm-leaf brought a sudden, sharp memory of the scent she used in her hair, paralysing him for a moment. But steeling himself, he broke it open, unfolded the simple palm-leaf and read what it said:

'My lord, I pray you will accept this letter and bear with my importunity. I am grieved that I should have caused you and your noble wife to leave this city at night without even the permission of your parents. Forgive me this sin. I know you to be true and honourable.'

Madhavi was changed, yes, but she was Madhavi still. He had suspected her of guile and blamed her for the way his life had gone, but in her way she had always been true. Of course Kavundi was right; he alone was responsible for his actions and for the consequences of those actions. But what misery he had brought about for everyone!

He decided he must go on to Madurai, as he had planned, and start a new life. There could, of course, be no further communication with Madhavi. She would understand. As for his parents, perhaps Madhavi's letter would at least explain the situation.

'Give this letter to my parents,' he said. 'Tell them I bow before their lotus feet and beg them not to grieve over my absence. Go now, go quickly Kausikan!'

When the Brahman had gone, he felt a great sense of relief as if he had finally shaken free of Puhar and the last of his attachment to Madhavi. He was free now to begin again. He brought the water to Kannagi and Kavundi.

When he returned to his wife and to the *sadhvi*, he was smiling, and soon afterwards when a band of wandering minstrels stopped in the same place, he actually borrowed a *yaal* so that he could join them in their singing and dancing. His mood was infectious, soon Kannagi was laughing, and even Kavundi could not help enjoying the scene. Later, Kovalan asked the minstrels how far they were from Madurai.

39

'My dear sir,' said the leader of the troupe, speaking with elaborate gestures, 'Can you not feel the southern breeze blowing from that very city? Can you not, even now, smell the scent of flowers from its gardens, of delicious spices from its food stalls, of smoke from its sacrificial fires? No, it is not far — perhaps a day's walking. And the roads are safe, for you are now in the Pandya country, under the protection of King Nedunchezhiyan.'

They rested during the day and walked during the night. And this was the last night of all, for in the morning, to their amazement and delight, they heard the distant sound of drums from the royal palace and the sacred temples of Madurai, sounding the morning hour! More sounds reached them as they walked on nearer and nearer — the chanting of early morning prayers, the trumpeting of elephants, the neighing of horses and the songs of the war-bards.

At last they reached the banks of the Vaigai, Madurai's own river, praised and sung by so many poets. Across, on the southern bank, they could see the city walls of Madurai with its four famous gates. Banners were streaming, bearing the Pandya emblem of the fish. At their feet lay the river, glinting in the morning sunlight, covered with fallen blossom. The travellers could feel their weariness falling away and Kannagi exclaimed with delight, 'Why, it is a river of flowers!'

4

The Anklet

The sun rose higher. It would be a brilliantly hot day. They could see the landing stages along the river, where large ferry boats were moored, with their bright and decorated prows, some shaped like horse-heads, others like the heads of lions or elephants. Crowds were beginning to gather along both banks of the river, passengers wishing to go to and from Madurai. But Kavundi preferred to avoid the crowds, so they walked some distance along the river-side before they asked a boatman to take them across.

They walked along the city walls, a little awed, feeling almost as pilgrims do when they circle holy places. Kavundi then led them towards the eastern gate. Here, outside the city walls, there was a small settlement, a group of simple bamboo huts set amidst tall coconut and areca palms. The place was well-known, for a community of ascetics, people who had devoted themselves to religion, lived there. This was Kavundi's destination. Here she would seek out sages who would direct her further in her chosen path.

Kavundi knew that the time had come for Kovalan and Kannagi to go their own way. It was best so; her concern for them could go no further. But all the same, she could not look forward to parting from these two who had become very dear to her. She was glad when the community waived its strict rules and offered the young couple hospitality for the rest of the day and a night, but she withdrew from them and retired to the hut which had been allotted to her.

The next morning Kovalan woke with a start, the drums of the town from palace and temple sounding loudly in his ears. He remembered that the journey was over. Thoughts came rushing into his head. They were just outside Madurai, the new life he had promised himself was within reach. He was full of excitement. At the same time he was aware of several practical problems. Where was he to begin? He looked at Kannagi who was just beginning to stir. He said softly to her, 'I'll be back in a minute,' and went to see Kavundi.

Kavundi adigal was at her meditation, but she looked up at the young man. Suddenly he bowed before her as he had done on that first day at the hermitage outside Puhar.

'When my wife and I first came to you,' he said, 'you asked us why we were travelling like destitutes. I did not wish to say anything then. Perhaps by now you know already. Nevertheless, I wish to tell you this. I once did a great wrong to my wife; she was hurt, and suffered a great deal. I wanted to take her away from Puhar, but that has meant the cruelty of this long and arduous journey. It is now my responsibility to re-make our life together. I must go into the city to seek out merchants known to my father who may be able to help me. Dear saint, you have been our protector all these days. May I leave my wife with you for one last day?'

'My son Kovalan,' said Kavundi, 'I know nothing of the sorrows of love and of parting, for all my life I have sought to free myself from these attachments. As for me, I admire the sages who are above all desires and are untouched by the world and its ways. But I do know that you are not the first to suffer in this way. Neither are you entirely to blame, for love brings suffering. Think of Lord Rama, who, obeying the commands of his father, went into exile with his wife. There in the forest he lost her and suffered untold grief for a time. Was he to blame, he who is wisdom itself? And what of Nala who lost his kingdom at a game of dice and fled to the forest with his wife Damayanti, and there abandoned her one dark night? Think of what Damayanti suffered. Yet was she to blame? No, my son. Think yourself at least more fortunate than these, for your beautiful wife is always with you. Come, do not grieve. Go into the city and make your enquiries. Come back to us when you have found a home. Kannagi will be with me.'

She smiled at him. He hurried back to tell Kannagi and then turned towards the city gates.

Densely packed thorny trees as well as high walls surrounded the city, securely protecting it against invaders. The eastern gate was vast, wide enough and tall enough for elephants to enter. Tall, fair-skinned men stood guard on either side, with drawn swords held in their hands. Yavanas, thought Kovalan. He had met Yavana merchants in Puhar, for Masattuvan, his father, worked with a few of them, but here apparently the Pandya King employed them as guards too. He glanced at them curiously, but they took no notice of him.

Now the city spread out in front of him and he walked along a wide street which took him to the centre where the palace and the temples were.

Madurai was undoubtedly the most famous of the ancient cities in the Tamil country at this time. It was famous for many things—for

42

its beautifully designed towers which gave it its other name, Nan-madak-kudal or cluster of four towers; for its poets and its assemblies of learning; and for the prowess and justice and its king, Nedunchezhiyan. So many times during his journey southwards, Kovalan had been told of the Pandya King's protection and care. To his subjects it was like the cool shade of the high-held white umbrella that always accompanied the King. He was even more famous for the unswerving impartiality of his justice, symbolised by the uprightness of his sceptre, his *kol*.

Perhaps this was true, thought Kovalan, glancing towards the heavily guarded doors of the palace gates, but what had struck him most of all as he walked along, were the immediate signs of wealth and opulence in the city. So many people seemed to be leading lives of ease and luxury. For he had noticed many good-looking women, dressed in all their finery, adorned with fresh flower garlands entwined with pearls, out for walks in the early morning. Some accompanied their menfolk in the pleasure gardens which bordered the river Vaigai, some were in the pleasure boats on the river.

He noticed next, walking back along the main street, the many flags and banners streaming in the morning breeze. Flags floated out from temples, from shops and warehouses, each bearing itsown device. It seemed almost as if the city were decked out for a festival. Well, he should be able to distinguish the different kinds of merchandise in the city easily enough. But where should he begin? Whom should he go to? He was passing by some vast mansions which he took to be merchants' houses. They were two or three storeys high, with many balconies and windows. He paused before a heavy wooden door, carved with lions' heads.

'I am the son of Masattuvan, pearl merchant of Puhar...' he tried the words out to himself. But how was he to explain his present condition? No, no, he could not do it. He could not bring further dishonour to his father's house than he had already done. He decided on an impulse that he would not seek out his father's associates as yet. He must make a beginning by himself. Later he would meet them with pride.

He had walked past the street of the merchant houses now. Strains of music floated out to him. A morning music lesson was in progress in the street of the courtesans. The deep voice of the music teacher was followed by the thin, reedy singing of a young girl, going over and over certain scales. Poor child, she would never make a very good singer.

He left the residential area behind him, passed the great open market, and came to the traders' streets, one for each kind of merchandise. He walked fairly quickly past the grain merchants. There were great sacks of pepper and of different kinds of grain heaped about — paddy, millets, peas, sesame seeds. They spoke of the prosperity of the Pandya country, but they also meant inland trade and Kovalan knew nothing about that. The clothiers' shops attracted him a little more because of the brilliant colours of the great bales of cotton, silk and wool, but he still walked on until he reached the jewellers' street. Here he paused and walked slowly, looking at the gems winking in the sunlight — diamonds, emeralds, sapphires and rubies. And semi-precious stones — lapis-lazuli, topaz, onyx, many-hued opals and branching pink coral. He lingered in front of a pearl merchant's. He gave the trays of creamy and pink pearls a searching look. Not one that he could see showed a single flaw caused by sand, wind or sea-water. Should he go in? At that moment the merchant at the counter looked up and saw him. An expression as of impatience and suspicion crossed the man's face. Kovalan walked on.

44

He came to the goldsmiths' street. Little flags in front of each shop proclaimed the kind of gold out of the four known varieties used there. Each displayed finely crafted ornaments—necklaces, rings, bracelets. But Kovalan knew that Kannagi's anklets were better than any of these. He could see nothing to match their workmanship here. They would certainly fetch a good price, he thought to himself, becoming suddenly practical. That was where he would begin. He must approach a goldsmith himself.

He walked on and on until the sun became too hot to bear. He had certainly confirmed his hope that Madurai was a rich and prosperous city with flourishing trade. He thought that within a few days he should have realised some capital. He would then be in a position to begin his own trade. But meanwhile he and Kannagi did not have a home for the night.

Kannagi had spent a quiet day with Kavundi. They had seen few people thoughout the day. However, towards late afternoon, a pleasant old woman named Madari, who belonged to the cowherd clan, stopped to talk to them. She had the weatherbeaten face of one who has spent most of her life outdoors. Having always lived in Madurai, she knew this area like the back of her hand, the best places for grazing, the small shrines in the open fields which she had visited since she was a child. In fact, she was on her way to one such shrine that very moment; it was her practice to take an offering of milk there every day. And of course, she liked to pay her respects to the holy men and women on the way, she said, touching Kavundi's feet.

45

Soon after Madari had left, Kovalan returned. He was tired, but began to tell them immediately and at some length, of the various splendid sights he had seen in the town, and of Madurai's prosperity, which he attributed to the wise government of Pandyan Nedunchezhiyan. But he said nothing about having found lodgings. Kavundi was puzzled.

The light was beginning to fade. A newcomer to the community, a Brahman named Madalan passed by.

'Why, it is Kovalan, son of the great pearl-merchant, Masattuvan,' he said. 'I wonder if you remember me? I was once among a group of Brahmans whom you feasted.' It had been during the naming ceremony of little Manimekalai, but Madalan did not wish to recall the occasion 'Alas,' he went on, 'you look as if your fortune has changed, you who once were so generous to others. Perhaps it's the result of some error in a former life.'

Kovalan began to look troubled, and Kavundi quickly interposed, 'It would not be proper for you two to stay here for another night. You know that this is a strict community and only ascetics and religious mendicants find shelter here. You are of the world, and it is right you should return to it. Kovalan, can you not find a place to stay in the city? I am sure some merchant, hearing who you are, will be only too pleased to offer you hospitality. Go quickly, before it gets dark.'

But Kovalan hesitated and looked even more troubled. Kavundi looked at Kannagi, still weary after her long journey. If only she, Kannagi, could be assured of even a temporary home! She looked out of the bamboo hut and saw Madari returning that way from her daily errand. In a moment the old woman had stopped to bow to the *sadhvi*.

Kavundi thought of the blameless lives cowherds normally lead, looking after their animals, and offering their produce to the gods and to men. Moreover, this old woman, Madari, had a special air of innocence about her. She seemed kind and virtuous. Kavundi felt she could trust her to look after Kannagi.

'Madari,' she said, resolving Kovalan's problem for him, 'look at these young people here. When the rich merchants of this city come to know who they are, and the name of this girl's father-in-law, they will want to accept them into their homes at once as honoured guests. But until such a time, I entrust her to your care.'

Madari looked surprised, and Kavundi continued,

'Take her home with you now. Give her water for a bath and a freshly washed garment to wear. Let her put *kohl* to the ends of her eyes once more and dress her hair with flowers. She is a woman of noble birth and it is time for her to resume her position in society. Be a guardian to her and a mother, but be her servant too. For many days, Madari, the elements have been pitiless towards her. Yet throughout her long journey she has had no thoughts for herself. Such love and faithfulness as hers are truly god-given. Take her with you now, go quickly.'

Kavundi took Kannagi's hand and placed it in Madari's. 'Goodbye, my child, god go with you.'

'Come,' said Madari simply, accepting Kavundi adigal's charge without question. 'Come, young mistress, it's getting towards time to milk the cows. My daughter Ayyai will be waiting. You'll like her.' They both bowed to Kavundi, Kannagi silently touching the *sadhvi's* feet.

Kovalan was the last to leave. 'I shall remember you and your words always,' he said. She blessed him and returned to her cell and to her meditations. Her responsibility towards them was over.

The sun was setting as Madari brought the young couple through the eastern gate to that part of Madurai where the cowherds lived. It was the hour when shepherds and cowherds were returning from grazing their animals, the herds moving hazily through the evening dust which was luminous with the last of the light. The air was full of lowing and bleating. The men carried some of the smallest lambs across their shoulders; some had curved sickles and staves from which hung pots of milk.

Madari chatted endlessly as they walked along, stopping every now and then to greet people she knew, to stroke a calf or a lamb, or to ask after her favourite animals. At last she brought them to a small cottage whose walls were washed with red earth, and which was neatly fenced off with a thorny hedge.

'This is my house,' she said, with obvious pride, 'and you must stay here, sir and lady, for I can easily move in with my daughter, Ayyai. She lives just next door and I spend most of my time with her anyway. O, here she comes.' She turned to the handsome, dark-skinned girl who had just joined them and who was looking at the visitors with some astonishment. Ayyai had known her mother to bring home a lamb with a torn leg, a bird with a broken wing, or a squirrel with a hurt paw. She was always doing this. But this evening she seemed to have outdone herself.

Madari, guessing her daughter's thoughts, said quickly, 'Ayyai, these are good people, newcomers to Madurai, whom a holy woman has given in my charge. Look, the lady is exhausted. Help me to get some water ready for her bath and some clean clothes. And look, they must be famished.'

'I should like,' said Kannagi, 'to cook the evening meal for my husband myself, if you will be generous enough to give me some rice and vegetables.'

'Of course, of course! And Ayyai will help you. But come in, come in and have your bath first.'

By the time Kannagi had emerged from her bath, fresh and clean, Madari and Ayyai had laid out for her, new cooking vessels, cucumber, breadfruit, mangoes, bananas and pomegranates, fine white rice and fresh milk. Each one of their friends had contributed something for the newcomers. Ayyai had even lit the small cooking fire in the courtyard. Madari greeted her guest.

'Young one, how beautiful you look! You really put to shame the painted city women one sees in Madurai. Look now, everything is ready for you, and I will leave. You are in a safe place, lady. We will look after you, my treasure, my golden one. The *sadhvi* need have no worries about you.'

48

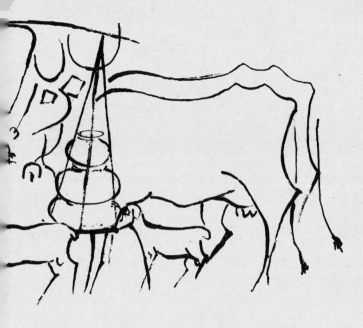

Kannagi thanked her and set to work. All through the journey, the
travellers had eaten what food they could get. Sometimes
monasteries and temples had fed them, sometimes the villagers and
peasants or other travellers had shared with them what they had.
Sometimes they had just lived on fruit. It was a long time since she
had cooked and served Kovalan a meal. It seemed a new and real
beginning. She was not even aware that her eyes were smarting from
the small, smoky straw fire. Deftly she sliced fruit and vegtables,
carefully she drained the rice.

When all was ready, she went through all the customary rituals
she had been taught, and which she had loved to do when Kovalan
and she were first married. She laid a small, neatly woven palm leaf
mat for Kovalan to sit on, and brought a pot of water to wash his
feet. It was a simple earthenware pot, but served just as well as one
of the fine silver ones she would have used at home. Next she
sprinkled water on the floor in front of him, patted it with her hands,
and then placed a green plantain leaf on which she served the rice.
Almost formally she said, 'Your food is served, my lord, will you
eat?' Kovalan, taking his cue from her, repeated the prayers proper
to the merchant community and then began to eat.

It was thus that Madari and Ayyai saw them from a distance,

passing by that way to see if they had everything they needed. Ayyai put her hand on her mother's arm to stop her going in, and murmured, 'They look so peaceful, mother. Don't disturb them.'

'I wasn't going to,' said Madari indignantly. 'But I have such an odd fancy. Shall I tell you who they remind me of? He looks just like Krishna when he lived among the cowherds. And isn't she like Yashoda who rescued and looked after him? I can't look at them enough, you know.'

'Yes, yes, but come away now,' and Ayyai led the old woman away.

They finished eating. Kannagi handed Kovalan a betel leaf folded over betel nuts to complete the meal.

'Come and sit by me,' he said. When she had done so, he began, 'There are still so many things I don't understand. My life seems like a dream, a troubled dream. I can't make sense of it. Why did I act as I did? Was it a cruel game of fate? I've wasted so many of my years on trivial things. I've failed my parents, and I've failed you. And now I have dragged you all the way here. Could there be any hope for someone like me? Yet when I asked you to leave Puhar and go with me, you did so immediately. Tell me, Kannagi, how were you able to do it?'

She broke her silence at last over all those years of loneliness. 'I just want to say this, and then I shall never speak again about that time. There were two things that hurt me most of all. First that I could not honour Brahmans nor give hospitality to religious men and to our relatives in your absence. In this way we failed to keep up our family traditions. Then there were your parents. How often they visited me and expressed their love and concern! Yet I could not be open with them. They were even more distressed by that, I think, because they could see through my pathetic efforts at cheerfulness.

'I will answer your last question though.' She looked up and met his eyes directly. 'It is true, I could not praise the life you led. But neither could I change my life and what I had chosen to be. I believed in you and so I followed you.'

'You astonish me,' he said. 'Here you are alone and poor in a new city, but you are still the same. You make a home out of nothing. You put courage in my hands. I shall go into town first thing tomorrow, taking one of your anklets. Our luck must turn now.'

It was early the next morning. Kannagi brought her husband a fresh flower garland. He chose two jasmines out of it for her hair. Then he embraced her and set off carrying the anklet carefully

50

wrapped in a piece of white cloth. He hated leaving her alone, although he knew that Madari and Ayyai would always be by her side. He took a last look at her, standing by the cottage door, and then walked swiftly past the cowherd settlement. He was making for the jewellers' street which he had already located the previous day.

He had been wondering how to approach a reliable goldsmith, as he had already rejected the idea of first finding one of his father's friends. But as soon as he turned into the goldsmiths' street it looked as if he was in luck. For suddenly he saw a master goldsmith in court-dress in front of him, walking in the direction of the palace, followed at some distance by a procession of assistants. Kovalan caught up with the young men and touched one of them by the arm. 'Whom does your master work for?' he asked, just to make certain.

'My dear young man,' answered the assistant haughtily, 'my master works for none other than the King and Queen. He is from the Chera country and is a newcomer to Madurai, but Queen Koperundevi thinks he is the finest craftsman she has ever met.'

This was enough for Kovalan. Swiftly he went up to the master goldsmith and said, 'Sir, can you value for me an anklet fit to be worn by the Queen herself?'

The goldsmith stopped short and looked Kovalan up and down with some surprise and suspicion. The young man looked poorly dressed, but he had a proud and noble bearing. A strange look passed over the goldsmith's face and he said with exaggerated politeness, folding his hands, 'I'm not exactly inexperienced, for I make a few trifling crown jewels for the King and Queen.'

'Well, please look at this,' said Kovalan, bringing out his cloth packet.

'Hush,' the goldsmith put his hand over the packet, stopping Kovalan. 'Not here, my dear sir. Let us be more discreet.' He raised his voice to his assistants. 'I have some business to attend to; wait for me.'

He hurried Kovalan down a lane and led him to a small deserted shrine. 'Now let me see.'

Kovalan unwrapped the gold anklet and was gratified to see the look of absolute astonishment on the goldsmith's face. The anklet was superb. It was made of the finest gold, known as *kilichirai*, parrot's wing, because of its greenish tinge. It was engraved most beautifully to represent a garland of flowers and leaves, and was embossed with rubies and diamonds. Although it looked solid to the eye, in fact, it was hollow, filled with little jewels which tinkled to Kannagi's steps. The goldsmith examined it minutely, his eyes

gleaming. He lifted it to his ears. Finally he said.

'This is most extraordinary. I have never seen anything to equal this except at the workshop of my master in distant Vanji. Do you know, by any chance, where it was made?'

'I think my wife's mother had a goldsmith from Chera Nadu,' said Kovalan.

'Yes, yes, that would explain it. What astounding luck! I mean the Queen will be delighted by a piece like this. She's a most fastidious lady. You were right, of course, it's quite worthy of the Queen. But who would have thought of it!' He seemed quite overwhelmed by the beauty of the anklet. 'Sir,' he said, turning to Kovalan, 'you see that I am on my way to the palace. Let me speak to the King straightaway. I will come back soon and we will speak about a price. Wait for me here please. Don't go away on any account.' And he hurried off, leaving Kovalan wondering at the swiftness with which events were moving.

About two months before, Pandyan Nedunchezhiyan had decided to give his wife, Koperundevi, a gift of a pair of anklets. The Queen

52

was often jealous of the time he spent away from her, and every now and then he tried to placate her with a lavish gift. She was usually delighted by these attentions.

The recently appointed goldsmith was commissioned to design the most beautiful pair of anklets he could. He knew perfectly well what to do. After all, he had carried in his mind for more than ten years a design he was longing to execute.

As a young man, he had been apprenticed to a master goldsmith at Vanji, the Chera capital. A brilliant craftsman this goldsmith was. Although at that time he was very old, the jewels he made were so exquisite, the traceries so finely drawn, it was impossible to believe that human hands had made them. The young man had been particularly delighted by a pair of anklets that his master had recently made. They were beautifully shaped, set with diamonds and rubies. How he had loved to hold them in his hands, letting his fingers learn each groove in the stylised flowers and leaves, the placing of each winking gem, the way the clasp worked over the heel! He would lift the anklets to his ears, listening to the smooth tumble of the gems inside, he imagined them as a cascade of rolling pearls. The master craftsman had once come upon him like this. 'My son,' he had said, 'have a care. It is well to love beautiful things, but do not let them possess you.' It was soon after this that the anklets had gone to a merchant prince's lady in distant Puhar. In time the apprentice had become a master craftsman in his own right. His fingers had almost the same skill that the old man had had. And in his mind he carried the design he would make one day.

He made the anklets himself, refusing the help of any of his assistants. He found he could remember each minute detail. When they were finished, he knew they were his, not Koperundevi's. He would never let them go.

Certainly he brought them on the appointed day. He fitted them on the queen's ankles, his hands lingering on the clasp a shade longer than stricly necessary, so that she drew her slender feet sharply back, almost kicking him away.

A few days later, one of the anklets was missing.

The Queen suspected the goldsmith immediately. After all, he had access to her jewels. Only recently had he come to polish some antique and valuable pieces she had. Besides she never got over the sudden repulsion that she had felt as he had fitted those anklets. Now she said that she had never liked him and his unpleasant manner.

Nedunchezhiyan, however, refused to be swayed by her feelings. The goldsmith was always accompanied by his assistants, he said, and there were always maids in attendance upon the Queen. How could he have had the opportunity? The goldsmith was unlikely to jeopardise his career by risking a theft of his own work. Besides, the maids also had access to the jewels. What could be more likely than that one of them had taken it? Pandyan justice, said the King, a little pompously, demanded that he should not act without sufficient evidence.

There was suspicion and ill-feeling in the court. Quarrels arose easily between the girls who attended the Queen. The Queen used to taunt Nedunchezhiyan for dragging his feet over the affair. He ought at least to hold a proper enquiry, she said. He owed her that much.

The goldsmith knew that sooner or later, this was just what would happen. He had indeed stolen the anklet and hidden it where he thought no one could find it. As a last resort, he could always melt it down. But he would die rather than let it come to that.

It was when things had reached this stage that Kovalan chanced to meet the goldsmith with Kannagi's anklet. Even through his extreme astonishment and delight at seeing once more his old master's workmanship, it came to him with a shocking light that here was a way of extricating himself. The theft could be, must be, pinned on Kovalan.

He hurried back along a little lane to the main street. He told his assistants to wait for him a little longer and walked towards the palace alone.

The King was seated in the audience hall, watching a court performance of dance and song. The occasion was not going too well. The troupe was only a mediocre one, Nedunchezhiyan saw that in the first few minutes after they had entered his presence. He was courteous all the same and would sit through the whole sorry performance. However, his attention began to wander very soon, and his eyes began idly to pick out the prettier young girls. Koperundevi, seated next to the King, was well aware that he was not seriously watching the performance. She was already annoyed with him over the affair of the anklet, and now she chose to take his wandering attention as an oblique insult to her. She rustled to her feet haughtily. 'My lord, I have a headache. I hope you will excuse

54

me if I leave now.' And she swept out, followed by her maids.

Nedunchezhiyan could not with good grace follow her immediately. It was a court performance, after all; his minister and courtiers were there on invitation. But he sat there with mounting irritation until it dragged to an end. Even then, there were courtesies to be exchanged. At last the visitors left, and he hurried towards the Queen's private chambers, determined to put an end to the wretched quarrel once and for all.

The goldsmith entered the audience hall just as the performance was ending. He followed the King along palace corridors, sidling along the ornamental pillars, finally running up to him as he reached the heavily guarded and locked doors of the Queen's chambers. Falling at the King's feet, he praised him, with the hundred forms of address that a commoner usually used in the royal presence.

'My sovereign lord,' he said, coming at last to the point, 'you will, I hope, be pleased to hear that the thief who stole my royal mistress' anklet has been found.'

'Well, go on, go on, don't stop there, man,' said the king impatiently. 'Who is this fellow? And how do you know all this?'

'My lord, he is a young man of almost unbelievable guile and cunning. Imagine, he doesn't carry any tools — pickaxes or crowbars or anything like that. How he got into the heavily guarded palace is a mystery. He has been in hiding for some days, emerging only last night to make a raid on my workshop. I have managed to persuade him that I am on his side, and he is hiding now at a shrine very near my house. He has the anklet on his person, my lord, I have seen it myself. There can be no doubt that he is the thief. But he is desperate and needs to be handled carefully.'

'We'll see about that straightaway,' said Nedunchezhiyan, sending for three of his strongest palace guards. They arrived in haste, strapping big men, all three. Two of them were older men. They were not particularly clever or imaginative, but they were long trusted servants of the King and certainly good at obeying commands. The third was a young man, something of a lout, but of unblemished courage. He had been resting after the night patrol, and had to have a quick drink when summoned, to keep himself awake.

Nedunchezhiyan beckoned to one of the Queen's guards as well. 'Go with the goldsmith,' he commanded all four of them. 'See if the thief has the Queen's anklet in his possession. If that is really so, kill him immediately and bring me the jewel to the Queen's chambers.

And he stepped forward to find Koperundevi, confident that their quarrel was over at last.

Kovalan sat in the small shrine, happy that his troubles were ending. He was fortunate that the goldsmith was acting so quickly on his behalf He shut his eyes and gave himself up to thoughts of what he must do next, how best to invest his money. He was interrupted by the sound of footsteps. He opened his eyes and looked up to see the guards towering above him. Was something wrong? He

56

looked from one to another in some surprise.

The goldsmith spoke, 'These soldiers are here, under orders from the King to look at the anklet.' His voice was as silky as ever, but there was a touch of menace in it.

Kovalan silently drew out the anklet and the guards bent over it. The goldsmith touched the Queen's guard's arm. 'See the design like a wreath of flowers? And look how the diamonds and rubies are placed at the centre of the flowers. Notice how the clasp fits together like two halves of a flower, with the fine screw heads fitting into the design.' The Queen's guard nodded, convinced. It was the Queen's anklet, all right. But he looked at Kovalan in some consternation and then drew the goldsmith aside. The other guards followed them, leaving Kovalan where he was, wondering what was happening, but not really alarmed.

'The man doesn't look like a criminal, nor does he act like one. How can we kill him?' The other three had apparently chosen this man as their leader, and were agreeing with him.

'But my dear fellow,' said the goldsmith smiling a little contemptuously, 'how did he come by the anklet? Can you explain that? Thieves are adept at deceit and disguise, as you very well know. You must not be so simple-minded as to be taken in by them. At this very moment while you are dithering here, and laying yourselves open to the King's displeasure, he is probably hatching one of his plans. Heaven knows what he uses — drugs, incantations? By the

57

way, did any of you palace guards trace the thief who stole the King's younger brother's diamond necklace not so long ago? According to some of you, he went through a number of disguises, didn't he? First he stood outside the palace doors dressed as a foreign courtier, then he gained access to the royal chambers disguised as an attendant. Never did catch him, did you? Vanished, you said, as if by magic. Even the prince ended up battling against a pillar. Well, it may have been magic. They are clever, these fellows. And I tell you, that one behind us is the cleverest of the lot.'

One of the palace guards said suddenly, 'Yes, they are cunning, these thieves. I remember meeting one of them on my rounds, one dark and rainy night. This burglar suddenly appeared before me, just like a black tiger. I drew my sword, but he snatched it away from my hand in an instant and was gone. I say, come on, we must decide what to do, the King is waiting.'

'I am waiting,' said Kovalan behind them. They swung round. The youngest guard, still unclear about what was happening, lurched forward and flung out his sword. It pierced Kovalan instantly. He fell, his bright blood spurting to stain the floor of the small shrine.

5

Kannagi in Madurai

Soon after Kovalan had left the cowherds' settlement, even while the great morning gongs were sounding in the city's palace and temples, Madari came out of her cottage. She found Kannagi standing outside, binding into her hair the flowers which her husband had handed her from his garland as he left. 'You slept well, I hope?' asked Madari. 'I expect the young master has gone into the city already,' she went on. 'Young lady, don't fret. We'll not let you be lonely. Would you like to come and watch us make butter? It is an important day for Ayyai and me, our turn to take butter and *ghee* to the royal household. Each of us must take our turn to supply the King's kitchens, you know. Ayyai is bringing the churning cord and stick.'

But in a few minutes, Ayyai came running out in great distress, followed by some of the other girls from the settlement. Ayyai, usually so calm and practical, called out in a fluster, 'Mother, something is wrong — something is very wrong. The milk which I put in the pans last night hasn't curdled at all. We shall not be able to make fresh butter. Perhaps we should use yesterday's butter for the *ghee*, but I'm finding it difficult to melt it. And have you seen the animals? No? Well, come and look at the animals!.'

Madari and Kannagi followed her hurriedly to the back of the cottages where the cattle sheds were. 'Look, mother,' Ayyai pointed out, 'the cows are all huddling together, shivering. The bulls have slipped off their bells, goodness knows how! And why are the lambs so quiet? It is very strange. What could have gone wrong?'

Madari did not like what she saw. Among the people who herded cows, tears in bulls' eyes and their bells falling to the ground were thought to be evil omens; it was the same with milk that refused to curdle and butter that would not melt. She walked up to the cows, however, and patted them soothingly. 'Something has frightened them,' she murmured. She sent one of the girls to see what they could do for the palace needs. Then she said, 'Look, Ayyai, first we must calm the animals. Let us dance the Kuravai. That will gladden them and it will please Kannagi. And it will also propitiate the gods and call down their mercy.'

The *Kuravai* or love-dance was a favourite among the cow-girls, and was always performed on special occasions. It showed the games that Lord Krishna and his elder brother Balarama played with the milkmaids, and especially with pretty Pinnai of the long dark eyes. 'Come, come,' called Madari, naming the seven girls who were to take part, three of whom would represent Krishna, Balarama and Pinnai. The seven came forward, clasped hands to make a ring, and began dancing in perfect rhythm, recreating the sports of their favourite god who once lived among the cowherds.

The vague fears of the early morning receded as the girls took up the rhythm of song and dance. Kannagi watched entranced. Madari, who never failed to be transported by the sight of the Kuravai, suddenly called out in a strange mood of exaltation, 'Sing, sing! Sing the praises of him who rides the Garuda.' And the girls, catching the old woman's mood, raised their voices together:

> Sea-coloured god, long ago you churned the ocean-depths,
> The northern mountain your pestle, the great snake
> > Vasuki your rope.
> Yet Yashoda imprisoned those hands with a churning cord.
> Lord, you who wear the lotus, how shall I fathom this mystery?
>
> Changeless one, all the gods worship you and sing your praises,
> You who swallowed the entire universe.
> Yet, in play, you stole the butter from the cowherds' churns.
> Lord of the *tulasi*-garland, how shall I fathom this mystery?
>
> Lord Tirumal, in two strides your lotus feet
> Encompassed the three worlds and banished darkness.
> Yet those feet walked this earth, messengers for the Pandavas.
> Lion-god! How shall I fathom your mystery?

The ritual series of dances had not yet ended, but Madari left the young girls and went to bathe in the river Vaigai and then to worship Lord Vishnu with flowers, incense and sandalwood. It was late morning by the time she finished her worship and returned home. It was then that a young girl who had been selling milk in the city saw her from a distance and came running after her. This girl had heard what had happened in the little shrine off the goldsmiths' street, and was anxious to break the news first to Madari and Ayyai. But by the time she caught up with Madari, the old lady had already reached the circle of cow-girls. There they were, still flushed and laughing. Kannagi was sitting next to Ayyai.

The cow-girl burst in upon this scene, pale and panting. Her eyes circled round and stopped short at Kannagi. Horror was in that gaze, she could not speak a word.

Kannagi looked back at her, and instantly her head began to swim. She turned and clung to Ayyai. 'My husband hasn't come back yet. Ayyai, my friend, I feel ill, my breath comes fast. Look, the sun is high in the sky, yet I am shivering. Why hasn't he returned? Ayyai, help me, what is it? What is she hiding from me? Speak to me, Ayyai.'

'Tell her,' said Ayyai to the newcomer.

'They took him to be the thief who stole the gold anklet from the palace. The soldiers have killed him under orders from the King.'

Kannagi could hardly take in what the girl was blurting out. Words, in isolation, seemed to hit her. Thief? Her husband a thief? She leaped to her feet, her face pale with anger at the insult to Kovalan. Then a great wave of sorrow overcame her. That anklet — hers alone and freely given to Kovalan — was a pledge between her and her husband. A pledge of faith and renewal. O god, what had they done? He was dead. She collapsed, weeping wildly.

After some time her voice rose in a lamentation of grief and rage, overwhelming rage at the injustice, at the slur upon his honour and at her own helplessness. 'O what shall I do now,' she cried out, 'my beloved husband is dead, murdered by this unjust and blundering King. How can I consent to bear it all humbly and meekly? Am I to be as abject and useless as those widows who can only make terrible vows at their husbands' funeral pyres? He loved me and he is dead. How am I to live a half-life without him, making futile pilgrimages to holy rivers?'

The silent cow-girls stood and watched with awe as she rose to her feet after some time. She had changed; she looked as if her anger alone was holding her up. She walked straight to the centre of their circle, and called out in a loud ringing voice, 'Listen to me all you who gathered here to dance the Kuravai. Oh, you were right to read the ill omens this morning. In your presence I call upon the Sun God whose rays are pure flame and who sees everything on this wide world. Speak to me, now, O god, and bear witness. Was my husband a thief?'

Into the silence, a voice directly replied, 'He was no thief. Lady, this city which accuses him shall be destroyed by fire.'

After the Sun God had spoken, Kannagi, as if divinely inspired, her face blazing with anger, made straight towards the city, stopping only to fetch her other anklet. She held it high in her hand, and as she strode along, she called out, 'If there are any virtuous women living in this city which is ruled by an unrighteous King, come now and listen to me. Listen to this injustice. Today, this morning, I have suffered unspeakable sorrow. My husband was never a thief; the anklet in his possession was mine. They killed him in order to take it away. Have you ever heard of such iniquity? Oh, even if I should see my beloved husband now, I can never hear him defend himself. How can this be justice? Alas, there is no comfort for me anymore.'

63

People came out into the street of Madurai and were amazed to see her walking alone, distracted, wild with anguish, yet with unmistakable pride and dignity. Helpless, knowing that any attempt at consoling her would be in vain, they said to each other, 'If the King is really the cause of an innocent woman's sorrow, then his sceptre is bent forever. What is to happen now? If the honour of the Pandya, King of Kings, bearer of the invincible sword, is shattered, what shall we do? If his umbrella of protection is no longer to be trusted, where shall we turn, what further mishap is in store for us?'

Some among the crowd were frightened and said, 'This woman looks as if she is possessed by a god. Did you notice her great strange eyes, reddened and streaked with tears?' Others again said, 'She has come among us like an angry goddess carrying her anklet of burnished gold. Heaven knows what this foretells.'

Someone had led Kannagi to the little shrine where Kovalan lay; it was the cow-girl who had brought the news of his death. Madari and Ayyai were still at her side, but walking as if in a trance she scarcely noticed them.

At last she saw him, still lying as the soldiers had left him in the pool of blood. She saw the gaping wound. She fell on her knees beside him.

The light began to dim. It was already evening. The women had all gone, leaving Kannagi alone with her grief. Only that morning he had handed her the flowers from his garland, and now, within the passing of a day, before the flowers could wither, he had died. And she was entirely alone. She spoke to him urgently in her thoughts, 'How can this be, how can it be right that your fair body should lie here in the dust! How can it be right that this garland should now be

drenched with blood! Alas, was it my own ill fate that brought this
about? Was it my own fate that led the Pandya to make such a tragic
mistake?'

The night wore on into a heavy still darkness, and even her grief
seemed to give way to a stony despair. 'Can there be women in this
city,' she wondered, 'or only such who will meekly bear any injustice
to their men? Are there no wise men here or only those who know
how to protect and look after their own? Is there even a god in this
city of Madurai where the King's sword is drawn against an innocent
man? How can there be a god here?'

She must have slept at last, her arms around his cold body. Quite suddenly he seemed to rise and lean over her. He wiped away her tears with a gentle hand and said, 'Your bright face looks dimmed.' In an instant she was clasping his feet with both hands, crying with relief. But he had risen only to leave her at last and for ever. And as he joined the spirits of the other world, his last words to her were, 'My dearest, you must stay here.'

She sat up and thought. Had it been an illusion? What else could it have been? Was some spirit tormenting her? O, where could she seek the truth? She had no further desire to live, but she would not join her husband until she had defended his honour by shaming the unjust King.

As she rose to her feet, she remembered her dream of long ago which she had once recounted to her friend Devandi in Puhar. Vivid flashes of it came back to her—the city which they had entered, hand in hand; the false accusation against Kovalan; herself challenging the King. Terror and violence. She was inside the nightmare now. Without wiping her face or binding up her hair she made her way to the huge gateway of the Pandya palace.

At the Queen's apartments in the Pandya palace, Koperundevi woke up that morning with a start, raised her head from her silken pillows and called out to her maids. 'O, what terrible dreams, what terrible dreams I have had! I saw the sceptre bending and the white umbrella falling down. The great bell of justice at the palace gates was ringing by itself. My heart seemed to shake with fear. My god, all round me, in all eight directions, it seemed things were wavering and falling apart. The rainbow was shining in the night and meteors fell by day. O, these are ill omens, evil omens! Help me, I must go in and tell the King.'

Her attendant maids hurried to her side to calm and reassure her. They adorned her in her favourite jewels and clothes; they brought her auspicious things such as incense and silk to avert the evil. Ready at last and resplendent as usual, she went towards the audience hall. She was followed by her retinue of dwarfs, hunchbacks and women in waiting, all walking in solemn procession and calling out in chorus, 'May you live long, Queen of the noble Pandya, royal consort of him who protects the whole wide world.'

The King was already in the audience hall, seated on the lion throne. He looked like the favourite of Lakshmi, Goddess of Fortune, as he smiled at her in welcome. How could she have supposed that any harm could touch him? She ran to him to tell him of her evil dream and to be comforted by him.

At that very moment Kannagi reached the palace gates and called aloud, 'Doorkeeper! O guardsman to an ignorant King who has failed in his duty! Go and tell your master that I wait at his gates. Tell him I am a woman who has lost her husband. Tell him I carry in my hand a single anklet out of a pair.'

The doorkeepers were startled and even a little frightened. She seemed such a slim, small figure, yet they could see that she was absolutely determined. There was no question of arguing with her or reproving her. After a moment's conference one of them went in to the audience hall. He bowed before the Pandya. 'Long live the King of Korkai,' he said 'Long live the sovereign of the southern kingdom who never stooped to an unrighteous deed! My lord, a woman waits at the gates wishing to see you. She says she has lost her husband, and she is standing there in a terrible fury, looking like the goddess Kali or Korravai. She carries a gold anklet in her hand.'

A gold anklet again! Nedunchezhiyan guessed that it would be the thief's wife with some made-up story and a series of complaints. This would have to be sorted out. 'Well, I will see her,' he said, graciously. 'Bring her in here.'

66

She came in, a strange sight in that hall of splendour and luxury. She was still wearing the simple cotton clothes that Madari had provided her. Even with her hair loose and dishevelled, her face pale and washed with tears, she carried with her an air of nobility. With firm steps she walked up to the throne and stood before the King, slim and straight as a spear.

He felt a strange tug of compassion for her, and said gently, 'Young woman, I can see from your tear-stained face that your are very unhappy. Who are you? What do you wish to say to me?'

She looked straight at him with blazing eyes. 'O you rash King,' she said, 'I have indeed a great deal to say to you. I come from Puhar, famous for the justice of its rulers. You know of the great King Sibi, who cut off the flesh from his own body in order to save a dove. You have heard how Manunithikanda Chola sacrificed his own son under the chariot wheel because he was guilty of killing a calf. My husband, Kovalan, was born in such a city, in the family of the

renowned merchant Masattuvan. His lineage is one of unstained honour. He entered this city with my anklet, which he wished to sell in order to earn an honest living. It was he whom you — in your injustice — ordered your soldiers to kill. I am his widow, Kannagi.'

Nedunchezhiyan found his compassion giving way to irritation. However, he told himself that the woman was half distracted with grief, and forced his voice to remain calm. 'Lady' he said, 'it is no injustice to order the death of a thief. On the contrary, it is the rightful duty of a King.'

'King of Korkai,' she returned, loudly and firmly, 'in this case you were certainly not doing your rightful duty. I say he was not a thief. O, I will, I must convince you. The anklet is mine. I can prove that it is mine. My anklets are filled with rubies.'

'Well spoken at last,' he replied, seeing a way of ending the case. 'Our anklets are filled with pearls. This can be verified soon enough.' Turning to the Queen, he added 'Send for the anklet which was found on the thief.'

Koperundevi who had been listening to this exchange, silent and amazed, now despatched one of her maids to bring the gold anklet which she had not yet put away. A few minutes passed during which no one was at ease except Kannagi. The court waited, tense and silent. The maid came running back and placed the anklet she had brought at the Kings feet. Kannagi stepped forward and placed the one she had been holding all this while next to it. The two anklets gleamed, perfectly matched, making a pair for all to see. The assembled court drew a sharp breath. Doubts began to assail Nedunchezhiyan's mind.

Then Kannagi reached for the anklet that the maid had brought, lifted it high, and with one swift movement broke it into two. Rubies, bright as blood, spattered out, some even striking the King's face.

68

The King stared aghast, the blood draining away from his face. He knew that he could no longer claim for his emblems, the sceptre of justice and the umbrella of protection. 'It is I who am the thief then,' he said, 'for I acted on the words of the goldsmith without thought. I am no King, for the honour of the Pandyas, protectors of the southern kingdom, is tarnished through me, now and forever. It is best that I should die.' After these words he seemed to collapse in a huddle on the throne. Koperundevi sank in a silken heap at his feet, whispering only, 'What consolation can one offer to a woman who has lost her husband?'

But Kannagi towered above them still, and when she spoke again, her voice was stern and sharp. 'Lady,' she said, turning to the Queen at last, 'Fate has been cruel to me, as it has to you. I am only an ignorant woman, and there are many things I do not understand. But one thing I do know. If you should wrong someone in the early morning, you will surely be called into account before the end of the day. I must tell you too that I come from a city that is renowned for the steadfast loyalty of its women. I need remind you only of princess Adimandi, daughter of King Karikala. It is said of her that she jumped into the foaming sea when her husband was carried away by the waves. She stood there, calling after him and refusing to move until the King of the Sea himself returned her husband to her arms. Such are the women of my country. And if I am one of them, a daughter of Puhar, loyal and true, I cannot allow either this city or its sovereign to survive.' And she turned her back upon the court and strode out of the palace.

The great city of Madurai was before her, throbbing with life. Flags streamed from the trading houses and temples. Shops were open, filled with goods. Pleasure-seekers walked the parks. The streets were thronged with crowds. She noticed nothing. She walked through the city, calling out aloud as she went, 'Hear me, men and women of this city of Madurai, famed for its four soaring towers! Listen to me, you gods in heaven! I curse this city because its ruler killed my husband wrongfully. I declare to you that I am free of blame.' Some among the crowd followed her, filled with foreboding, other were too absorbed in their own business to notice.

Three times she walked round the city, pronouncing her solemn curse. Then she wrenched off her left breast and flung it from her, into the dust of the city.

Immediately the God of Fire stood before her. He looked like a Brahman priest, but his body was as blue as embers bursting into flame; his dishevelled hair stood out in red points. When he spoke, his teeth shone, milk-white. 'Woman of unstained virtue, long ago I was commanded to destroy this city on the very day that it wronged you. Therefore order me now. Whom do you wish to spare?'

A swift thought came to her of the kindness of the holy men and women, of the innocence and generosity of Madari and Ayyai. She said, 'Spare the priests and all virtuous men. Spare faithful women, old people, children and cows. But do not on any account spare the wicked.'

Instantly the fire started, beginning from the palace itself. Smoke began to spill out from the royal apartments into the corridors and

70

reached the audience hall. At first the courtiers and ministers, the women in waiting and all the assembled court stood still. They were trembling with fear but were still awaiting orders, unaware that the King and Queen were already dead. Then as tongues of flame began to lick the walls, they fled in panic. As the fire reached the courtyards and stables, frightened elephants and horses began to trumpet and shriek; guards, soldiers and stable-keepers abandoned duty and made for the gates, some making a futile attempt to beat back the flames, others bent on saving their lives alone.

The fire began to race along the streets, leaping from roof to roof and catching along the wooden balconies. It was time for the deities of the four groups of the inhabitants of Madurai to act. The first of these was of the priestly order. He was a moon-coloured god, wearing clothes which were ritually pure, and the sacred thread; he was well-versed in all the priestly rituals. The second was of the order of Kings. He was coral-coloured and was clad in red silk, adorned with many fine ornaments; he wore a royal crown. The third was of the order of merchants; himself golden-hued, he was dressed in golden brocade. The fourth and last was revered by the craftsmen of the city; his body was dark blue, his ornaments were silver and his wreath was made of all the wild flowers of land and water. The four now met and said to each other, 'From ancient days we have known that on the day the King of this land failed to render justice, this city would be doomed to destruction. It is time for us to leave.' And so they left, slamming the gates of the city behind them as they went.

The fire raged and enveloped the whole city. Flames rose high above the great mansions; ornate balconies and heavy teak doors caved in and crashed down. Small stalls and hawkers' stands were burnt to ashes, while the big warehouses and the great temple cart itself were ablaze. The residential parts of the city were in tumult, the air thick with belching smoke and falling soot. Children woke up screaming with fear and rushed out, clutching at their mothers' hands; old women faltered out, stumbling as they went. Dancing girls and musicians abandoned their musical instruments, and scholars their precious manuscripts. Elephants and horses rampaged along, wild with fright, and managed to reach beyond the city walls. From the cowherds' streets, Madari, Ayyai and all the gentle cow-folk herded their animals into safety. It was the wise ones alone who knew that the true reason for the fire was Kannagi's torn and flaming breast — and they found in her no cause to blame.

The fire raged on until the houses of luxury were laid low, the temples, the theatres and the palace all in ruins. The city was at last abandoned, its festivals and celebrations gone, its worship and rituals finished. Its streets were dead and still except for the few crackling flames; dark and dead except for the last smouldering embers.

Kannagi alone stumbled on through the streets and byways, destitute, wretched, in a stupor of grief. She did not even realise completely what was happening about her.

There was no one else left in the city except the tutelary deity, guardian and protector of the royal house of Pandya. She too walked the streets, for she would not desert Madurai. She was a goddess of many aspects, combining both beautiful and feminine as well as fierce and war-like qualities. Though the left side of her body was deep, dark blue, her right was gold-coloured. In her left hand she held a golden lotus, but in her right she brandished an awesome and fearful sword. On her right foot she wore the heavy anklet of victory as soldiers do, but on her left a slender and uniquely worked anklet sounded.

The goddess shadowed Kannagi for a while, and at last spoke to her from a distance. Gently she said, 'Lady, will you listen to what I say?'

Kannagi's once beautiful face was sad as she turned with some exasperation and asked, 'Who are you to follow me like this? How could you know what I suffer?'

'My friend,' said the goddess, 'of course I know how deeply you suffer because of the death of your husband. But I ask you also to understand my own pain for the Kings I protect. As guardian and goddess of the Kings of Korkai, I must prove to you the honour of the Pandya Kings who always deeply regretted and atoned for any injustice that could be laid at their charge.

'Please listen while I tell you this story. At one time, long ago, there was a great scholar, Parasaran, well-known for the brilliance of his logic and disputation. Once, while travelling through the Pandya kingdom, this Parasaran stopped to rest at the Brahman village, Tangal. There, seeing the Brahman boys at play, he offered a prize to the child who could best repeat after him certain Vedic chants. The youngest of them all, a little boy called Alamar Selvan, son of the priest Vartigan, repeated the great Parasaran's words with faultless accent. The scholar was delighted by this performance, gave the child many beautiful pieces of jewellery, and then left. Soon after

this, the village watchman, jealous perhaps of Vartigan's newfound wealth, accused him of misappropriating a hidden treasure which should legally belong to the King. So the priest was imprisoned. Then Kartikai, the wife of Vartigan, furious at the injustice, called out many curses. And the goddess Korravai, hearing her, refused to open the doors of her temple in Madurai to any of her worshippers.

'The reigning Pandya immediately sent his men to find out in what way he had offended the goddess. In this way he came to know about Vartigan. Sending for the priest, he admitted to him that his officers had been at fault, and compensated him handsomely for the humiliation he had suffered. But the Pandya also expected to be forgiven.

'Kannagi, I must tell you that in all the days of the reign of King Nedunchezhiyan, I have never heard the bell of justice ringing for anyone in distress; this city was filled only with the sound of the chanting of prayers. I do not wish to deny that the King was sometimes at fault. But don't you think he merited forgiveness?'

Kannagi said nothing. The goddess was silent for a while. After some time she went on, 'Now let me tell you about your husband's past life and why this tragedy happened to him. Many years ago, in the Kalinga country, there were two rival princes, Vasu of Singapuram and Kumara of Kapilapuram. There was always suspicion and jealousy between these two. An unknown merchant by the name of Sangaman came to the city of Singapuram with his wife Nili. In all innocence, wishing only to make money honestly, he set up shop in the market-place. Unfortunately, one of King Vasu's agents, Bharatan by name, overzealous in his duty, mistook the newcomer for a spy sent by the rival King. Bharatan brought Sangaman before King Vasu, accused him and killed him. Thereafter, Nili, Sangaman's wife, cursed Bharatan for wrongfully accusing her husband. Fourteen days later, still in rage and despair, she threw herself off a cliff and died.'

74

'Listen to what I have to say now, and give up your anger. In a former life your husband was the same Bharatan who made that fatal mistake and you yourself were the desperate Nili who cursed him. This is your tragedy. A virtuous life is good in itself, but it may not prevent the sins of a past life from bearing fruit. Alas, this is the law of life. Be calm now; still your anger. What is more, I may tell you this. In fourteen days you will meet your husband in his heavenly form, for you will never see his earthly body again.'

Kannagi still said nothing. Nor did she feel anything. Even her anger ebbed away. The fire had at last abated. The goddess turned and left. At last Kannagi spoke. 'There is nothing left for me now. But I shall neither rest nor sleep until I see my husband again.'

Slowly she too turned and walked towards the city gates. At the doors of the temple of Korravai she stopped, went in and broke her bangles in token of her widowhood. Then she walked through the ruined city and reached its western gates. She said quietly, 'I entered Madurai through its eastern gates with my beloved husband; and now I leave it by the western gates, alone.'

She wandered on, neither aware of day nor of night, desolate. The river Vaigai flowed along in flood, she stumbled along its northern bank, through ditches and canals, always walking westwards. She began climbing a hill which was sacred to the god Murugan. She had left the Pandya kingdom behind and come to the borders of the western kingdom which was ruled by the Chera kings.

Hill tribes lived here among the thickly wooded slopes. The girls came out in groups, singing and laughing as they went to bathe in the mountain streams. Wild birds wheeled about and monkeys chattered to her from the treetops. She stopped and leaned against a flowering *vengai* tree. She looked about her and suddenly said aloud, 'I am a woman who has done a terrible deed.'

Fourteen days passed by. She looked up to see blossoms raining upon her in a celestial shower. The gods encircled her, singing and calling her name. Kovalan beckoned from their midst. Eagerly she rose and went with him to the other world.

6
Cheran Senguttuvan's Expedition

After the death of Karikala, the Chola King, Senguttuvan of the Cheras became known as the mightiest of the southern kings. The Chera country lay along the western coast of southern India, and its capital was at Vanji, on the banks of the river Periyar, not far from the foothills of the western mountains. There, in his silver palace the great Cheran Senguttuvan sat one day with his Queen Venmal, looking out into his gardens. Senguttuvan was famed as an invincible warrior and he was seldom long in his own country, but now he was in an unusually peaceful and joyous mood. As he watched the crystal fountains playing in the gardens, he felt a sudden impulse to visit his hills, to see the endless forests enshrouded in mist and cloud, and to hear the rushing waterfalls. Acting on his impulse, he set out from Vanji on his elephant, with the Queen and courtiers, and made for the Cenkunru hill where he camped on the banks of the river.

It was beautiful there. The river descended from the mountains in cascades like the necklace of god Tirumal. Round about them the royal party could hear the hill people singing the praises of their favourite god, Murugan, as they harvested their small fields of millet. The voices of the young girls were fresh and clear:

> You who speak sweet words, my friend,
> We have bathed together in the cold mountain streams
> Until our eyes were stinging and red.
> Let us praise our beautiful god Murugan,
> Who slew the *asura* with his lance.
> Come, let us dance the Kuravai and sing.
>
> He lives in Tiruchendil and in Tiruchengodu,
> He lives on the high white hill and in Erakam.
> He carries the brave lance, leaf shaped, resplendent.
> He once entered the ocean and slew the *asura*
> Who stood in the water like a mango tree.

High above the songs arose the call of hunters looking for wild honeycomb. In the distance wild elephants trumpeted in the dense forest, and sometimes tigers roared.

Very soon the hill-folk realised that the royal court of Vanji had come into their midst, and hastened to offer their respects. The village headmen came in procession, bearing on their heads the produce of the mountains as presents for the King and Queen. They brought with them white tusks of elephants, bundles of sweet-smelling *aghil* wood, whisks of stag hair, sandalwood, cardamom and pepper, fresh coconuts, mangoes, huge jackfruit, hill plantains, strings of garlic, sugarcane and flower garlands. Some carried with them the young of mountain animals: tiger-cubs, lion-cubs, musk-deer, parrots, peacocks and monkeys.

When they had spread their offerings at the feet of the Chera King and Queen who received them all with gracious thanks, one of the village headmen stepped forward. 'For seven births we have been your subjects,' he said, 'may you be ever victorious, great King! We wish to tell you of a strange thing that happened in these parts. Not long ago we saw a young woman with a single breast sitting alone in the forest, under a *vengai* tree. It seemed to us that she was in great pain and suffering deeply. Yet as we crossed the millet field where we were working and approached her, we were astonished to see that she was received by a host of gods and carried into the other world. Where she came from and whose daughter she was, we cannot imagine. Live long, my lord, and reign over us for a hundred thousand years.'

Senguttuvan was surprised by the headman's news and wondered aloud who the strange woman could be. At this point, a brilliant and learned poet by the name of Sattanar who had recently come on a visit to the court of Vanji from his own city of Madurai, leaned forward to speak to the King. Sattanar had been listening to the headman's account with keen interest and now said, 'My sovereign lord, I can tell you about this remarkable woman.' He went on to relate the events of the tragedy at Madurai. 'Perhaps,' he concluded, 'Kannagi wished to point out to you the injustice she suffered under the Pandya king. It is strange that she did not wish to return to her own country, but found shelter at last in the Chera land.'

The story had a profound effect on both King and Queen. It seemed to bring home to Senguttuvan the duties and responsibilities of a King. 'It is good that the Pandya gave up his life willingly when he realised how unjust he had been,' he said, 'for in doing so he has straightened his sceptre again. Yet I do know that the career of a King is fraught with difficult decisions. He can never afford to forget the welfare of his people.'

To Queen Venmal, however, Kannagi seemed to be a divinely inspired woman. She said to Senguttuvan, 'I'm deeply moved to hear of the Pandya Queen who could not bear to be separated from her husband, and so died at his feet. Heaven will reward her. But my lord, I think that we should honour and celebrate this Kannagi who sought the border hills of our land. She deserves to be enshrined as the Goddess of Chastity and Steadfastness.'

Senguttuvan was pleased and inspired by the Queen's wish. As a man of action and quick decision, he immediately consulted his learned men and astrologers. They agreed that this would be a good thing to do. Kannagi should be commemorated as the Goddess of Steadfastness and a statue should be made of her which would then be consecrated. They said that it would be fitting for such a statue to be made of stone from the sacred Mount Podiyil and anointed in the river Kaveri. Or indeed the stone might be carved out of the great Himalayas and bathed in the river Ganga. For these were holy rivers and mountains and therefore pleasing to the gods.

By this time Senguttuvan was fired with enthusiasm. The idea of a great expedition took root in his mind. To fetch the stone from the neighbouring Mount Podiyil would not be a difficult feat for a King as famous and victorious as he. No, he would march northwards, joined by all his allies. Once in his youth he had brought his widowed mother Sonai, daughter of the famous Chola Karikala, to bathe in the sacred waters of the Ganga. He now proposed to cross the river and arrive at the very foothills of the Himalayas, doing battle with any of the northern princes who dared to stand in his way. There, upon the brow of the mountain he would carve his royal emblem, the bow, for all future generations to see. The stone would then be brought home in triumph. This would be the crowning achievement of his reign.

Senguttuvan returned to Vanji in haste with the royal party for he was anxious to begin his journey soon. A herald was sent out to make known the King's intentions to his people and to make certain that the foreign ambassadors in the capital would carry the message to their own countries. The herald went out on the royal elephant, beating his drum and calling out, 'Long live our King! Long may the great Chera protect us! Our King intends to march to Himalaya in

order to bring a sacred stone from which we will fashion the Goddess of Steadfastness. Therefore let all northern kings prepare to meet him with tribute. Let them remember all his valorous deeds and take heed to comply with his wishes!'

The Chera army, under the generalship of Villavankodai began to collect its forces. The great chariots, the war-elephants, the cavalry and the foot soldiers all began to assemble. Besides the army, astrologers, courtiers, bards and musicians were to go with Senguttuvan. At last the chief astrologer announced the auspicious hour when the march should begin. Immediately Senguttuvan ordered that the royal sword and the white umbrella should be carried northwards ahead of the hour, and places in readiness in the fort outside the town. As the royal insignia, wreathed with flowers, were carried out from the palace on elephants, people realised that the expedition was to start soon. The King's assembly called out auspicious blessings, warriors cheered deafeningly while war drums sounded and banners waved. That evening Senguttuvan held a great banquet for the army commanders.

Early the next day, the King himself left the palace. He walked alone to the temple to Shiva, wearing his wreath of Vanji flowers, emblems of the royal capital. Reverently, he offered his prayers to him who wears the crescent in his tangled hair, and received in return the blessings and victory tokens from the priests. Only then did he mount his war elephant and riding once through Vanji led his procession northwards. All the people left behind cheered as if it were Indra, ruler of the gods himself, riding into battle.

The huge procession stopped at the Nilagiri mountain first of all. Many people came to pay their homage to Senguttuvan here — dancers from Konkana, pilgrims and travellers eastwards, tribal people from Kudagu and Karnataka and many neighbouring princes and chieftains. Some of the travellers brought word that certain northern princes had begun to scoff at the Chera expedition, doubting whether they would ever reach the Himalayas. This infuriated Senguttuvan. Here he was at the outset of his journey and doubts were already being cast upon his success. His first mission must be to prove his honour.

Then Sanjaya was announced. He was a general in the service the Nurruvar Kannar, King of Magadha. He brought with him gifts and supplies, a consignment of troops, dancers and other entertainers. He also brought a friendly message from the Nurruvar Kannar, 'We have heard that our noble friend Senguttuvan is marching to the

Himalayas to fetch the sacred stone for the Goddess of Steadfastness. We will be pleased to accompany him on this expedition. We offer to bathe the stone-slab in the flowing Ganga.'

The embassy was timely. Realising that the purpose of his expedition had changed a little, Senguttuvan returned a message to his allies, 'We thank the Nurruvar Kannar for their kind greetings and offer of help. We have just heard that Vijaya and Kanaka, the two sons of Balakumara, have been so unwise as to speak ill of a Tamil King. We must tell you that this army marches with fury against those princes.' Senguttuvan then asked the Nurruvar Kannar to arrange for boats which would ferry his army across the great river.

Then, having acknowledged the tributes and gifts of his other allies, he continued his long march northward. At the Ganga, the Nurruvar Kannar had prepared the boats as they had been asked and themselves waited at the northern bank to welcome their friend. The Chera then marched on further and reached the kingdom of Uttarai where the hostile northern princes Vijaya and Kanaka had foregathered with their own allies. The enemy forces were as vast as the sea, waiting as if to test the prowess of the Tamil King. But Senguttuvan met the challenge with the joy of a hungry lion who at last sees a herd of prey in front of him.

The two armies met and clashed together, and high above the din the war drums sounded loud and long. The massacre was terrible, the battlefield a scene of carnage with hundreds of warriors dead, animals wounded, and once beautiful chariots crushed and splintered. At length the victorious Tamil warriors took Kanaka and Vijaya prisoner, together with fifty-two other chariot leaders. Senguttuvan had won. He then sent out a proclamation: 'We wish to assure all northern princes who follow the holy scriptures, protect the sacred fire and lead blameless lives that we honour them and desire to maintain peace.'

Then under command of the general Villavankodai, he sent a few of his troops further north to bring back the stone for the goddess.

The King had ordered that the stone should be carried upon the heads of the captive princes Vijaya and Kanaka as a token of their subjugation. It was first taken to the sacred river where it was ritually bathed, attended by priests and learned men. Then the king and his retinue made their way once more to the south bank of the Ganga. Here Senguttuvan rested in the beautiful palace set among fine gardens which his friends from the north had provided for him. Here too he gave rewards to all his victorious soldiers and prepared to meet the sons and families of the honoured dead.

While he was holding court, the Brahman Madalan suddenly appeared, and having first paid his respects to the King, went on to say, 'Is it not strange my lord King, that a story which began with Madhavi's sea-shore song should end in this way, bringing a heavy burden to the princes Vijaya and Kanaka?'

'Explain to us the meaning of your words, learned Brahman,' said Senguttuvan, 'for none of us present here understand your riddles.'

'I will tell you what I mean,' said Madalan. 'Once long ago, in Puhar, the actress Madhavi sang a series of sea-shore lyrics to Kovalan, intending to make up a lovers' quarrel. But the workings of fate are inexorable; the songs only drove them apart forever. Kovalan returned at last to his wife Kannagi and took her away with him to Madurai. You know of his tragic death there. Kannagi then entered the borders of your country alone, and it is for her sake that the northern princes today carry the stone upon their heads.'

'King of Kings, now let me tell you what brings me here. Sometime ago I left Puhar on a long pilgrimage to Mount Podiyil. Having reached the southern shores of the Tamil country, I bathed in the sacred waters of the Kanya Kumari and then turned homewards by way of Madurai where Pandyan Nedunchezhiyan then reigned. I met Kovalan, briefly there, and was indeed staying in the ascetics' quarter outside the eastern gate when all the events of which you have heard happened.'

'When we first heard that Kovalan was accused of stealing a gold anklet and then killed, Kavundi adigal was very angry. You must know that the young couple had become her spiritual wards during their journey to Madurai, especially Kovalan. She had, of course, insisted that they should leave her care —I was present when they left with Madari — but all the same she could not forget her concern for them. She felt most bitterly that Kovalan had been cruelly put to

82

death at the very time when he was starting a new life. News soon followed of the King's death and the terrible fire. Actually, although we ourselves were safe beyond the city gates, we could see the angry flames above the walls, sharp as the flickering of cobras' tongues. Kavundi then turned to those of us who knew her and said, 'Of course they had to see their fate to its end. I knew it and yet perhaps I could not accept it.' Then, having spoken to her religious teachers, she undertook a fast unto death as Jain renunciants sometimes do. And with the perfection of her penance, very much at peace, she died not many days later.

83

'I must tell you too, of Madari, the cow-woman. When the fire started, Madari's first care was the safety of her animals. She had a way with her, she could really calm down the frightened beasts. The cowherd and shepherds put together a makeshift refugee camp outside the city walls. As soon as they were all gathered together, Madari said to them, "You must know that Kovalan is blameless and that the King has made a tragic mistake. Yet if his sceptre is bent and the white umbrella forever shattered, I too have been at fault. For I failed to protect the girl who was given in my charge by a saint." So saying, she returned to the burning city in search of Kannagi, and perished in its flames.'

'After these terrible events and the utter ruin of Madurai, city of the Pandya who once rode a golden chariot, I returned at last to my own city of Puhar, bearing the ill news. When Massattuvan the pearl merchant heard all that had happened to his son, to his daughter-in-law and to the king of Madurai, he was overcome by a great sorrow. He insisted on giving away his vast wealth and entered the Buddhist monastery known as the Seven Viharas of Indra. There he is now one among the three hundred holy monks who pray daily for deliverance from the cycle of existence. But Massattuvan's wife died broken-hearted, she never recovered from the news of her son's tragedy. Manaykan, Kannagi's father, also distributed his wealth in charity and entered the order of Ajivika ascetics. Kannagi's mother died too, alas.'

You will want to know about Madhavi, once our finest and most brilliant dancer. For many months, ever since Kovalan's sudden departure from Puhar, she has blamed herself. She began to question the value of the sixty four arts and gradually gave up all public performances just as she had reached the height of her career. How Puhar missed those glorious occasions! When at last she heard of the tragedy and all its terrible consequences, she has decided to shave her

head and to receive instruction as a Buddhist recluse She now believes that it is desire alone that is the cause of this world's sorrow.

'Madhavi and Kovalan had a daughter, Manimekalai. Long ago I attended her naming ceremony. She is now growing up, and is very beautiful, with a kind of innocence that is very different from Madhavi's own brilliance. Her mother adores her and is determined she should never become a dancer. So ends a great line of dancers. Even the King mourns this decision.'

'As for me, after seeing all this, I have myself decided to make a pilgrimage to the Ganga and to bathe in its clear waters, for as a bearer of ill news I brought much sorrow to Puhar.'

Senguttuvan had followed Madalan's account with the greatest of interest. He sat lost in thought for some time. Then he asked, 'But

tell me further, Madalan, what has happened in the great Pandya country after its King died?'

'My lord King,' answered Madalan, after the sudden death of Nedunchezhiyan, the young prince Vetrivel Chezhiyan who was then at Korkai hastened to Madurai and was there crowned King. Soon after his accession he offered many sacrifices and prayers in order to propitiate the gods and at last freed the Pandya country from its disaster. He now reigns like the young sun newly risen in the sky. All is well in the southern kingdom.'

When Madalan was speaking to the King, it was gradually darkening outside. A vivid sunset burned low in the western sky and soon all but disappeared. In a few moments the crescent moon began to gleam among a few bright stars. And as the king raised his eyes to the night sky, the astrologer said quietly, My sovereign lord, it is now thirty-two months since we left Vanji.'

They were words Senguttuvan had been waiting for; he knew the astrologer's intent. It was time to return to his own land. He walked out alone into the encampment and along the street of the chariots. Around him the many tents holding his people were scattered over the plain, their dark shapes looking like small and large hills. It had been a long journey and a great and successful expedition. He walked on still, wondering about the strange way in which destinies of the three great Tamil Kingdoms had been linked together by the story of Kannagi. Slowly he returned to his apartments and sent for Madalan once more. He wanted to hear from him about the Chola country. The great King Karikala had died some time ago and his grandson Killi Valavan now reigned in Puhar. Senguttuvan himself had helped to establish his claims to the throne.

'How is it in the Chola country ,' he asked, 'now that the rebel chiefs have been put down? Does the new king rule with wisdom and justice?'

'I cannot foresee a time,' replied Madalan, 'when the descendants of the great Sibi should stray from the paths of justice. Our King Killi Valavan, ruler of the fertile Kavery plains, is indeed wise and just.'

Senguttuvan thanked the Brahman and gave him gifts. He then took leave of his northern allies, bidding them return to their own prosperous lands. Next he sent one of his generals, Nilan, to the Pandya and Chola courts where he was to exhibit the prisoners Vijaya and Kanaka. Then as the sun rose, filling the eastern sky with light, he mounted his elephant once more and led his victorious army southwards. Hearlds brought the news of the king's return throughout the Chera land. Soon the four regions of the country were ringing with ballads of his victory. In the hills, the Kurava girls sang as they drove away wild elephants from their millet fields,

> Make way for him who hastens home
> Wearing the garland of victory
> And for his swift-pacing elephant.

The ploughmen in the fields sang to their bullocks:

> He who trod down the walls of the northern kings
> And ploughed up their land with donkeys
> To sow white millet where once great fortresses stood,
> Our King, the ruler of the Kudavar has come.
> Tomorrow, my bullocks, you shall not wear your yokes
> For it is the birthday of our king
> And all prisoners shall be free.

Along the banks of the Porungai cowherds took up the theme as they played their flutes and sang to their cattle,

> Our ruler returns from the Himalayas
> he brings fine herds of cattle—
> soon you will have company.

The news spread like wildfire as far as the coast, to the sailors and the fisherfolk.

Messengers brought the news to Queen Venmal who hastened to dress herself in her best bringing out her favourite silks and jewellery which she had put away for almost three years. Vanji was decked out with banners and streamers. Crowds began to line the streets to welcome home the warriors. And at last Senguttuvan entered the gates under his triumphant white umbrella, wearing the garland of victory.

For the next few days, Vanji was wild with joy. The women made thanks offering for the safe return of their warriors. The wounded were cared for lovingly, and every house lit its lamps and held a feast. Senguttuvan and Venmal took themselves to the wide terraced roofs of the palace where they were entertained with special dance performances and where they saw many royal guests.

In a few days, the general Nilan returned to Vanji with the captive princes. Madalan had decided not to remain in Puhar and came with him too. The general now reported that neither the Pandya nor the Chola Kings had shown any great signs of rejoicing at the sight of

86

the prisoners. Nor had they sent their congratulations as Senguttuvan had so confidently expected. On the contrary they had implied that the Chera's contemptuous treatment of his prioners was not worthy of a great and victorious warrior.

Senguttuvan laughed scornfully, but Madalan saw the anger leaping into his face dangerously and stepped forward at once. He had returned with Nilan for a special purpose.

'King of Kings,' he said, 'Long may you reign! You have fought many battles throughout your long life and your victories have always been great. You are like a lion among kings. I beg you to give up your anger now. And may your days be as numberless as the grains of sand that lie upon the banks of the Porunai. Now my sovereign lord, listen to my words and please do not brush them aside.'

'You, the great guardian of this land, are now over fifty years old, and though you have chosen to excel in the deeds of war, you have not as yet performed any of the royal sacrifices which are due to the gods. You have had many noble forbearers. Yet all those ancient heroes who once led armies, stormed fortresses and conquered new lands are now dead and gone. For life is fleeting, this body does not last. And wealth and power pass away—is that not abundantly clear in the defeat of these very Aryan princes who dared to scorn you? Nor need I remind you that youth and beauty are passing; you have seen the grey hair on your own chest.'

'You know that the lives of gods mays be incarnated in man, just as the souls which once inhabited the bodies of men may return again to this earth, housed in the outward form of animals. Our life a brief role which an actor assumes for the state; yet the sages tell us that it is our present actions alone which will decide which direction our souls will go next.'

88

'Mighty King, I speak these words to you, not because I hope for any rewards from you, but because I consider that you, a great man and a great King, should now turn your thoughts towards spiritual things. It is time for you to perform the great Rajasuya sacrifice which the scriptures prescribe. This will establish you as an Emperor and a King above all others who is pleasing to the gods. And I wish you to do it soon, for who is there in this whole wide world who may dare to say with certainty how long his days may last? Yet I pray that you and this your wise Queen may live long as guardians of this beautiful land.'

Senguttuvan listened to Madalan's words. He agreed that the Brahman, together with the other learned men of the Chera court, should arrange for the Rajasuya *yajna* to take place at Vanji as soon as possible. Moreover, a great temple was to be built, where the image of Kannagi, carved out of the stone-slab from the Himalayas would be installed. Finally Senguttuvan ordered that the princes Vijaya and Kanaka and all the prisoners of war should now be released. Villavankodai was asked to conduct the princes to a quiet place outside Vanji, where they were invited to stay until the last day of the sacrifice.

89

The consecration of the goddess was to be held on the first day of the Rajasuya sacrifice. Several days of ceremonies and other rites would follow until at last Senguttuvan would receive the imperial crown at the hands of the chief priest. Many royal visitors came to Vanji for the festivities. The northern princes who were freed would attend, of course, as well as the ruling princes of many of the neighbouring states, the Kings of Kudagu and Malava and King Gajabahu from distant Lanka.

There were, however, a group of women arriving from Madurai and Puhar, whom the king welcomed himself and escorted to the temple. These were Devandi and Ayyai who had befriended Kannagi in her worst moments of anguish, together with Kannagi's former nurse and her foster-sister.

It had been to Devandi alone that Kannagi had spoken of her pain at Kovalan's abandoning her, long ago in Puhar. Nor had Devandi forgotten the strange dream that Kannagi had recounted to her. At that time both of them had attempted to make light of it, but it had returned to haunt Devandi. Later, when she heard that Kovalan and Kannagi had disappeared from Pular, she alone with the old nurse

and foster-sister had followed her friend as far as Madurai. They arrived too late, after the tragedy, but there they met Ayyai. Ayyai was still heart-broken at that time, mourning the death of her kindly old mother and mourning the loss of her friend. The women had formed a close friendship. Together they made the journey to Vanji when they heard of the new temple to be consecrated to Kannagi, Goddess of Steadfastness.

A strange thing happened on the day of the consecration. As the rites were finished and the goddess enshrined in the beautiful temple, the King suddenly spoke out. The great warrior Senguttuvan was granted a vision. 'What is this,' he called out in wonder. 'What is it? Oh, what do I see? A woman appears in the sky, as brilliant as a lightning flash. She wears a jewelled girdle, her ears and wrists sparkle with diamonds. Gold circlets gleam at her ankles.'

Then Kannagi, for it was she, spoke to the assembled people. Her voice as it reached Devandi and Ayyai sounded incredibly happy, almost with a lilt of laughter, so that their anguish at last left then. 'The Pandya King,' said Kannagi, Goddess of Steadfastness, 'is no more to be blamed. Indeed he is now an honoured guest at the home of the gods and I am his daughter. I shall always be at this hill. My friends, will you not join me?'

In great reverence Senguttuvan and the royal visitors walked three times round the shrine, praying to the gods for prosperity in their lands. The King then arranged that floral offerings should be made to be goddess every day, with Devandi officiating at the shrine. After this he and Madalan, the Brahman, led the way to the sacrificial hall where the Rajasuya rites were to be held.

And in Vanji, the people rejoiced, praising equally the three great Tamil Kings:

90

> Long live the ancient dynasty of the Pandya,
> Long live the Kings of Madurai, encircled by the abundant waters of the Vaigai
> And blessed is the King who gave his own life
> Because of the sorrow that cruel fate brought upon a woman.
> Long live the ancient dynasty of the Chera,
> Long live the Kings of Vanji, engirdled by the flowing water of the Porunai
> And blessed is he who brought to us the daughter of the mountain
> Borne upon the heads of Kings.
> And let us all sing together
> Praising the Chola in whose land the Kaveri flows,
> The ruler of flower-filled Puhar.

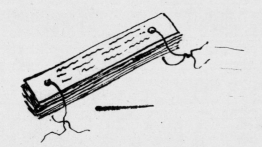

INTERLUDE
The poets and their story

Many years ago, when Nedun-cheral-Athan was the reigning King of the Chera country, an old astrologer came into the court of Vanji one day. The King was growing old then, but he sat with pride on the lion throne with his two sons by his side. The older prince had already distinguished himself in battle. Even now he wore the victory garland round his neck; one day he would be a great warrior. People speculated about the younger prince; he loved books and scholarship and he had many friends among poets and musicians, but he also spent much of his time with the Jain monks at Gunavayir Kottam. That morning the seer came up to the throne and paid his respects to the King. Then he looked long at the two brothers – with admiration at the one, with love at the other. Finally he pronounced that the younger prince would one day succeed to the throne: every feature in his face proclaimed it.

The young prince saw fury strike like a whiplash across his brother, Senguttuvan's face. He had seen that look before, he was to see it many times, again. It was the moment to make a decision which he had considered for some time. Almost instantly he said, 'This cannot be!' The determination in his voice silenced the astrologer. The he turned to the King and said, 'My father, I have decided to take the vows of the Nigranthya monks at Gunavayir Kottam. I wish to lay down the burdens of this worldly life and undertake with them the search for a far greater happiness. Give me you blessings, I beg you.'

From that very day Senguttuvan's younger brother left the place at Vanji and went to live in the monastery. In the course of time he took the Jain vows and came to be known as Ilanko adigal. As the younger prince, the name 'Ilanko' remained with him; he acquired the title of 'adigal' which was usually conferred upon ascetics. Not long after this the old king died and Senguttuvan was crowned King of the Cheras.

In renouncing all claims to the throne, Ilanko also saved his friendship with his quick-tempered brother, and it was a friendship that remained all their lives. Neither of the two interfered with the beliefs or the actions of the other; Senguttuvan remained a worshipper of Shiva all his life. Yet they met frequently, for the king always invited his younger brother to the royal court of Vanji when other learned visitors were present there.

Thus it was that when Senguttuvan went into the mountains and was told of Kannagi's arrival there, Ilanko was part of the royal party, along with Sattanar, the Buddhist from Madurai. Sattanar's story of the burning of Madurai inspired the royal brothers in different ways. Senguttuvan planned an expedition which would be both a display of his prowess and a token of his piety. Ilanko wanted to write a poem, setting out the strange story of love and tragic fate.

Ilanko spoke to his friend Sattanar about his plan. 'Indeed, yes,' said the poet from Madurai. 'I am sure that this story is a fit subject for a narrative poem. It tells of many truths: of kingly duty, of the power of chastity and steadfastness, and of the inevitability of fate. And since its matter will be of interest to all three crowned kings of the Tamil country, you, royal monk, familiar as you are with palace and monastery, would be fittest to be its author.'

So began Ilanko Adigal's work on the story of Kovalan Kannagi, which would be entitled *Silappadikaram*, naming it after Kannagi's anklet, her *silambu*. In the meantime Sattanar himself wrote a parallel, *The Renunciation of Manimekalai*.

Many months later, the final incident of Kannagi's story was enacted with the consecration of the temple at Vanji. As Senguttuvan led the way to the sacrificial hall, Madalan on one side of him and King Gajabahu of Lanka on the other, Ilanko was there too, the last in the procession to follow the ringing anklets of the victorious king.

92

Returning to his monastery, the monk who was once prince of the great Chera land wrote the last verses of his poem:

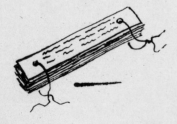

> Youth and wealth and this bodily life are all fleeting,
> Neither can you number the days of your life, nor escape your fate.
> Therefore seek only that which is good
> And so you may at last reach your goal of heaven.

Manimekalai

1

Manimekalai, Another Beginning

Once again it was the season of the Indra festival — twenty-eight days of celebration in honour of Indra the greatest of gods; a festival ordained by the sage Agastya himself. The festival drum was brought out by the town's hereditary drummer. He struck it as he rode about the streets of Puhar on his elephant.

Once again he called out, 'Long live this ancient city, beloved of the goddess. May the rains fall upon it three times in every month. May its King be always righteous and just.'

'Our sages tell us that all the gods will come down to this great city during the Indra festival, leaving the very heavens empty. Let us prepare to welcome them. Let us decorate our streets and our courtyards with banners, with filled water pots, with golden statuettes and tall lamps. People of Puhar, place auspicious banana trees laden with bunches of fruit at every street corner; also fresh sugar cane and flowering creepers. Wind strings of pearl around the golden pillars on your front courts that form a collonade along our streets. Spread white sand under the shady trees where people foregather. Be sure that you have observed all the appropriate rites to the high gods and to all the other gods. Let words of dharma be spoken to those who gather at our shrines and assemblies, teaching us the right path.'

'And for the twenty-eight days of the festival, when the gods will walk amongst us in our gardens, parks and lakes, may all hunger, disease and enmity cease.'

And so, in due course, the celebrations and festivities began. But it was a startlingly different festival this year. Neither Madhavi, still Puhar's most famous dancer, nor Manimekalai, the most promising of the younger women, made their appearance. Madhavi's mother Chitrapati was heart-broken, and also humiliated by the gossip that

came to her ears. Summoning Madhavi's friend and one-time maid Vasantamalai, she asked her to go and tell her daughter what the townsfolk were saying.

Vasantamalai also grieved over what she had heard : that Madhavi had renounced her former life. It was unthinkable that a dancer should do this. Therefore she agreed, only too eagerly, to go to the house in which Madhavi and her daughter still lived at this time. She found them in the little upstairs room. Madhavi, Manimekalai and another woman who had joined the now quiet household, were stringing flowers for worship. Taken aback by the changes obvious in Madhavi because of her recent penances, Vasantamalai spoke sorrowfully.

'Listen to me, Madhavi, you who are like the goddess Lakshmi herself. Has this town ever been hostile to you? Has it ever lacked in appreciation of you? Why must you turn your back upon it? As women of our clan and position, it is not right for us to give up our true destiny which is the celebration of courtly and popular dance. Nor should we ever forsake our skills in performing upon the flute, the drum and the *yaal* ; nor indeed our special knowledge of the sixty-four arts. Do you realise this, Madhavi? And do you know that the learned men of Puhar—just as much as the ordinary people— think it is a matter of shame for you to give up your true vocation in order to follow this ridiculous path of renunciation?'

Madhavi said to her, 'Hear me first, Vasantamalai. When I came to know of the dreadful tragedy my lover, Kovalan, experienced, and when I found myself left with this life that refused to leave my body, at that moment I renounced whatever fame or prestige I have gained in this town of Puhar. But at the same moment, I renounced shame, too. So do not speak to me about the honour of our clan, it means nothing to me. As for Manimekalai, let me tell you this. It is well known that many virtuous women, on the death of their husbands, die instantly of sorrow. Or they enter the funeral pyres of their husbands. Or they at least undergo the fierce austerities of widowhood, in the hope of being united with their husbands in the world to come. But our Kannagi chose none of these paths. No. She refused to bear submissively the evil that was done to her husband. She burnt down the Pandya capital of Madurai with the fire and flame of her own breast. Manimekalai is the daughter of that extraordinary woman — a virtuous and married woman. Therefore it is entirely appropriate for her to follow the righteous path of renunciation; more appropriate, indeed, than the lifestyle of a dancer.'

'There is something more. Listen, Vasantamalai. When I went to the sage Aravana adigal I was heartbroken and distraught. The words he gave me then were these: "Know these — to be born in this world is to experience sorrow. To end the cycle of birth is to achieve happiness. The first of these is the result of desire; the second is achieved by those who no longer are ensnared by desire."

'Then he taught me the four Noble Truths. These are— that all life is sorrowful ; that suffering is caused by ignorant craving ; that the end of suffering can indeed be achieved ; and that the way to that end is through the noble eight-fold path of right view, right aspiration, right speech, right conduct, right means of livelihood, right endeavour, right mindfulness and right contemplation.

'Aravana adigal also spoke to me of the tranquillity that can be achieved by observing the five *silas* or rules of conduct, that is, to refrain from destroying life, from lying, from stealing, from intoxicants, and from sexual misconduct. He told me to live by these rules alone.'

'Please tell my mother Chitrapati and our kinswomen all this.'

When Vasantamalai heard Madhavi's words, she grieved, the poet tells us, as if a priceless ruby had been tossed away into the foaming sea. She left Madhavi's house, sick at heart.

2

The Gardens of Uvavana

Manimekalai sat at her mother's feet, stringing flowers and listening to her tell the sad story of Kovalan and Kannagi. The words seemed to burn through her ears. Her heart melted with loving kindness, and tears streamed down her eyes, destroying the bright beauty of the kohl edging them and falling upon the flowers in her hands. It was a rare moment, the turning point when the result of good deeds in a past life began to bear fruit in this; like that instant, the poet says, when the scent that is deeply hidden within a flower suddenly and at once becomes discernible in the air. Upon that moment the stream of her life would turn.

Madhavi saw her daughter's tears and wiped them away gently. 'Dear child', she said, 'because of your tears these flowers have lost their purity. Go and gather some fresh ones and make a new garland.'

Sudhamati, the other woman in the room, had been working on the flower garland along with Manimekalai. She had been silent all this time. Now she spoke, quietly and sadly. 'If Manimekalai, with her beautiful face and her sorrowing dark eyes, sets off by herself, is it likely that the men of this city will leave her alone ? I ask this because of my own experience. You took me in when I came to your door, orphaned and homeless. You asked me no questions. But let me now tell my own story and how I came to be in Puhar.'

'I am the only daughter of the Brahman, Kausikan, from the sea-side city of Sambai. I grew up never afraid to be alone, with an innocent heart. One day I was gathering flowers in the city gardens, when a *vidyadhara* by the name of Marudavekan passed by. He was on his way to the great festival in Puhar, your own city, beloved of Indra and blessed by Lakshmi. He looked absolutely magnificent in his flower garland, his jewelled necklace and golden clothes. He had that divine appearance that seemed to invite the earthbound to worship him immediately. He gathered me up and I lay in his arms as he carried me up to the visible heaven of the lower gods. But then, in the time it takes to blink an eye, it seemed he had left me abandoned here, and disappeared into his own distant land.'

'No, Madhavi, it is best that Manimekalai does not go on her own to pick flowers. Besides, where will she go? The garden of Ilavantikai is full of the king's guards; and a kind guardian spirit watches over the garden of Uyyayana during the Indra festival. There are other gardens where she will not be able to enter.'

'But listen. There is the garden called Uvavana where the trees are always in flower by the command of the Lord Buddha whose love and compassion for all living things we know well, and whose life was one of unceasing search for the truth. Within this garden there is a crystal pavilion such that you may see the forms of the people who enter it, but cannot hear their voices. Inside that pavilion is a shrine that bears the footprints of the Buddha. Buds that are laid at that shrine may never open, and full blown flowers never fade nor invite bees. And Madhavi, I must tell you one more thing. If you place flowers there with your mind fully given over to a god, those flowers will surely reach that deity's feet. But if you put them there without any deity in mind, they will not move from that place. This is to prove that our deeds will not bear fruit unless they are intended. Now Uvavana is the best place for Manimekalai to go and gather flowers. Furthermore, I shall accompany her there.'

Madhavi was persuaded, and so the two young women went their way along the streets of Puhar. The streets were full of life, with the noise, the crowds, the sights of everyday.

A Jain ascetic walked past, naked, unwashed, mindful at all times of all living creatures, visible and invisible, and under a vow to eat only at certain times. Behind him came a man, very much the worse for drink, mocking the holy man elaborately, and offering him the blissful delights of both this world and the next, all of which, he claimed, were contained in palm wine. A crazed young man who had lost his wits, wearing tattered clothes held together with twigs, his body smeared with ashes, speaking unintelligible words came next. He wept, he fell about, he screamed, sometimes he twisted and turned, sometimes he lurked in corners, sometimes he fought with his own shadow. Some people followed him, watching his pitiful and meaningless actions. Then there came a troupe of women impersonators, decorated in knee-length skirts, dancing the 'pedu' dance, first said to have been performed by Pradyumna when he released his son Aniruddha from prison. Aniruddha was the son of

Pradyumna and grandson of Krishna. Usha, daughter of Bana fell in love with him and had him brought by magic influence to her apartments in her father's palace. Later he is discovered, rescued and a great battle ensued. Many in the crowded streets admired the murals painted on the outer brick walls of Puhar's grand houses, representations of the gods themselves, and of all living things, done on fine white plaster by the craftsmen of the city. Little children had been dressed and decked out in their heavy finery until the could hardly walk ; they had to be lifted onto little gilded chariots by their mothers who wished to take them to the celebrations in honour of god Murgan.

The two young women walked quietly past all these sights. Some people who recognised Manimekalai grumbled about her mother's cruelty in encouraging her daughter to follow the path of renunciation. Others remarked aloud on her outstanding beauty and her famed dancing and singing which was said to put to shame the gait of the swan, the grace of the peacock and the sweet tones of singing birds.

Taking no notice of all this, the two women walked on until they came to the dense trees and shrubs of Uvavana, covered with flowers. To their eyes it looked like a great canvas before them, painted in many colours. Sudhamati made a brief gesture of worship and led Manimekalai inside.

Sudhamati pointed out the many beauties of the park — its densely packed flower gardens, picked out by the light of dragon flies and brooded over by the twanging of bees; the *koels* wandering at will among the trees; the peacocks dancing. In the midst of a jewel-bright lake, spread over with lotus leaves and flowers, one lotus, the most perfect of them all, stood out, a royal swan riding it like a throne. And there on the banks of the lake, opposite the swan, a peacock danced, with the incomparable skill of a girl dancing in the royal presence, accompanied by the sweet song of the *koel* above, and the harsher counterpoint of the water fowls close by. In fact the lake was so overhung with flowering trees that the lotus blossoms on its surface were constantly dusted over with the falling pollen. About them and around them, kingfishers, blue as sapphire, darted after tumbling fish.

100

3

The Crystal Pavilion

The Chola King who reigned in Puhar was praised by all for his generosity as well as his justice, symbolised by his white umbrella and his sceptre. His only son, Udayakumaran was equally famed for his courage. Once, the famous battle elephant, Kalavekam, had run amok in the streets of Puhar, spreading terror all around. Like a ship wildly tossing at sea, it had suddenly thrown off its mount, and plunged among the ceremonial drummers who were walking in front, as usual. People shrieked as they sprang out of its way, for it had been like a mountain suddenly bearing down upon them. But Udayakumaran, hearing of the incident, had leapt on to his horse and hastened there, and had somehow managed to calm down the rampaging animal.

On this day he was riding along in his chariot, his hands touching its flower shaped ornamentation, his guards in attendance, looking like the god Murugan himself, but for the garland of *aati* flowers about his neck.

His chariot turned into the street of the dancers. There, in one of the large mansions decorated with gold leaf on its outer wall, by the window of a bedroom upstairs, he saw his friend, the merchant prince, Ettikumaran. The rich young man looked like an etching, so still and so sombre. His *yaal* was silent in his hands. His lover sat by him gravely.

The prince called up to him, 'Why, Ettikumaran, what could have happened to you to make you look so sad?'

Immediately the young man and woman came down and bowed to the prince. Ettikumaran said, 'My lord, I have just seen Madhavi's daughter Manimekalai on her way to the garden, her fresh beauty dimmed, like a flower that has been shut away in a box. When I saw her I instantly remembered the tragedy that struck my kinsman, Kovalan, and I was overcome with grief.'

But Udayakumaran only heard part of what Ettikumaran was saying. It was some months now since he had first seen Manimekalai dance. He was determined to win her, despite Madhavi's firm refusal

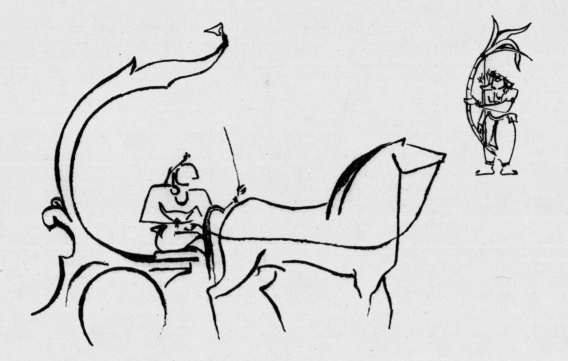

and despite the stories that he had heard of the changed lives of
mother and daughter. So she had gone to the Uvavana, had she? 'I'll
bring her back in this very chariot,' he said to his friend. And like the
moon slicing through massed and racing clouds he rode his chariot
in haste along the street and all the way up to the entrance of
the garden.

Now when she heard the clatter of those chariot-wheels coming
nearer and nearer, Manimekalai was washed over by a wave of
inexplicable feelings. She said to Sudhamati, 'I have a strange fear
that it is prince Udayakumaran's chariot-wheels that we are hearing
now. My grandmother, Chitrapati, has often sent Vasantamalai to
speak to my mother about this prince. She claims he has set his heart
upon me. Oh, Sudhamati, what shall I do?'

By this time they had reached the crystal pavilion. 'Go inside,
quick, and draw the bolt tight,' said Sudhamati. Then she herself
moved some distance away, taking up the position of an attendant.

Within minutes, Udayakumaran had arrived there. He stopped his
chariot and climbed down, leaving his guardsmen waiting. He came
up to Sudhamati and said, 'I know very well who you are, though you
stand there so quietly, all by yourself. Answer my question. Why has
Manimekalai left the street where her kinswomen and her community
live, and come here with you? What are you two doing here?'

Filled with dread, as if she had been cast down into the deepest of dungeons, Sudhamati said, 'Prince, you are a great Chola, descended from the line of the famed Karikala; I am an ordinary woman. What can I presume to say to you about true knowledge, or of dignity, or of princely conduct? Yet listen to this — that which is the result of our past *karma* will also be the cause of our future *karma*. Learn too about the limitations of this mortal life and the nature of this human body — stripped of all adornments it smells of flesh; it experiences old age, disease, and death; it is the receptacle of offences; it is the stranglehold of attachment; like a snakepit it is the dwelling place of anger; it is never free of helplessness, fainting and sorrow.'

Udayakumaran scarcely heard these words, for his eyes had caught a glimpse of Manimekalai, still as a coral statue, reflected through the crystal walls of the pavilion. At first he thought it was the image of Lakshmi in her form of the goddess of the Kolli mountains when she danced in front of the *asuras*. Then he realised that it was Manimekalai. He began to walk round the shining walls, his fingers groping against its smooth surface, searching for the door. He could not find it; in all directions he could see the same image, reflections of her. Frustrated, he called out to Sudhamati, 'Tell me, what sort of person is this young mistress of yours?'

Sudhamati answered quietly, 'You are young and as beautiful as the god Murugan. This is undoubtedly true. But she is not one to be moved by that. She is destined for a life of contemplation and austerities; the truths she seeks are proof against the arrows of Kama.'

Udayakumaran replied to her, ' I have to tell you that it is no more possible for me to give up my love than it would be to throw a dam across a river in full flood. You say that her life is to be given over to austerities. It makes no difference to my intentions.' With a jealous heart he was about to leave the place when he stopped suddenly. 'Wait', he said, 'are you not the young woman, much spoken of in Puhar, who was abandoned by a *vidyadhara* near a Jain monastery? Why did you leave that place, and how is it that you accompany Manimekalai now?'

'Oh prince', she said, 'live long, and learn to shun the path of evil. Yes, I will answer your question. I lost my mother early and was brought up by my father, a pious Brahman, who was getting on in years. When I was seduced away by Marudavekan and became entangled in a false marriage, my poor father grieved for me. He searched everywhere for me, setting off at last with a group of pilgrims who were bound for Kumari in the extreme south. While on his way there, he came with some of the Brahmans to bathe in the

104

holy place where the Kaveri joins the sea. And so at last, on the banks of the Kaveri, he found me alone and abandoned, in the city of Puhar. When he saw me, my father wept freely and said, "How is it my daughter that you are here, all alone?" Because he loved me, he would not forsake me, and because he chose not to abandon me, he had to abandon instead his life of teaching the scriptures. And so we lived here for a while as mendicants, begging for our daily food.

'One day as we were on our way home, a cow that had just calved sprang towards my father and gored him in the stomach. He was in an unbearable agony. Holding his entrails in his hands, he dragged himself to the nearby Jain monastery and called out, " Oh monks, I cast myself upon your mercy. Only you can save me now."

'But the monks came out and said, "There is no place for you here", and they gestured to me angrily to go away. We were both weeping by that time. "Will no one help us?" I called out desperately. "Is there no kind person here? Oh god, we are all alone."

'It was nearly midday. In that intense heat, a Buddhist monk appeared, wearing his saffron robes and carrying his begging bowl with which he had approached the tall merchant houses of Puhar, his face cool and merciful as the moon. With great compassion and love he asked, "What has afflicted you?" Then giving his begging bowl into my hand, he took up my father in his arms and quickly carried him to the house where his fellow monks lived. There, the sage, Sanga Dharman, healed my father's terrible wounds, and comforted and saved his life. It was after that that the monks sent me to seek out Madhavi.

'Taught by Sanga Dharman, I now seek only to praise the Buddha, the seat of all virtues, who lived only for others through several rebirths, who illuminated the path to *nirvana,* who set rolling for us the Wheel of Dharma with its spokes like the rays of compassion, who was victorious over Mara, the Evil One.'

'Very well,' said Udayakumaran, 'I know your story now. But it has nothing to do with my feelings for Manimekalai. I mean to possess her anyway. I shall ask Chitrapati, her grandmother to speak for me.' Saying this, he left the gardens and went his way.

Manimekalai came out of the crystal pavilion, saying to herself, 'Clearly he thinks that my piety is not to be taken seriously. He thinks I am still part of Chitrapati's clan, that I am willing to be bought by the highest bidder. Then how is it that my heart goes with him, forgetting his words? Oh mother, is this the nature of love? Then let me be free of its power.'

Now, at this time Manimekalai Devi, guardian deity of Kovalan's clan, who was in Puhar to attend the Indra festival, came to the shrine at the crystal pavilion disguised as one of the young women of the city. She walked around the shrine in devotion and then rose into the air, praising the Buddha and saying, 'You attained true knowledge and purity, ancient lord; you removed the three evils — destroying anger, enmity and delusion; you understood all things and were victorious over Mara. I have only one tongue to praise you who set rolling the Wheel of Dharma with its thousand spokes.'

And now, the day was ending in Puhar. The evening sky arched over the city's jewelled walls and domed temples, its streets and palaces. It seemed to be wearing the rising moon and the setting sun like two earrings, one gold and one silver. The evening cries of homing birds began to fill the air. Cows returned home, their udders heavy and flowing. As the petals of a large lotus closed over a swan, its mate freed it, ripping apart its flowery prison. Music sounded — a *yaal* playing a song of unfaithfulness in the *marutam* mode; a flute replying with a song of domestic bliss, in *mullai*. Women lit their household lamps and the Brahmans their sacred fires. At last dusk came, dark and sad, grieving for the sun like a woman whose husband has fallen in battle and who now returns to the parental home.

4

The Story of Chakkaravala Kottam

It was later still. The moonlight fell sheer, like milk from silver jars. Manimekalai Devi, who was like lightning released from a divine bow, bent low and worshipped at the shrine of the footprints of the Buddha, and then rose again, taking once more the form of a woman of that town. Now she turned to Sudhamati and asked her, 'What trouble has come to you? Why do you stand there, looking so desolate?'

When Sudhamati had related to her all that had happened on that momentous day, the goddess said, 'It is clear to me that Udayakumaran has not given up his love and desire for Manimekalai. He has left this garden for the moment, because he knows that it is a place that is set apart, a place that is frequented only by the pious. But I am sure that if you return through the main streets of Puhar, he will pursue you relentlessly. So what you must do is to go through the small western gate which opens out from these garden walls into the waste ground known as the Chakkaravala Kottam, or the Cosmic Place, where the most austere and rigorous of religious people live. You may safely spend the night there.'

Sudhamati said, 'Gentle goddess, the people of this city always speak of the place outside the western walls of this garden as the cremation grounds. How strange that only the false *vidyadhara*, Marudavekan, and now you, most beautiful one, call it the Chakkaravala Kottam. Please tell me why you give it that name.'

'Well, I will tell you that story even though it is now very near the darkest hour', said the goddess, 'and you and Manimekalai must listen carefully.'

She began by describing the cremation ground which had been there, next to the garden, ever since that ancient time when the city first came into being. It was surrounded by a guarded and fortified wall, with four gates. The waste ground served as both burial and cremation ground; it was covered with monuments to the dead in burnt clay, with different sections for different *varnas*. But it was a fearful place, a dwelling place of predatory birds and animals — the jackal, the horned owl and the man's-head bird — as well as demons and spirits. It was a desolate place; everywhere there were relics of the rituals of death — implements, discarded garlands, biers, smashed earthenware pots, rice-ball offerings. 'For death claimed all the citizens of Puhar impartially,' said the goddess, 'unconcerned whether they were wealthy or whether they had renounced all their worldly goods; whether they were young mothers or bereft children; old or young. Yet there were people who continued to live recklessly, as if in a drunken haze, unconcerned about leading good lives.'

She continued, 'Now one day, a young boy called Sarngalan walked into this waste ground, under the mistaken impression that it was a nearby fortified town. Instead he heard terrible noises proclaiming death ; the howling of a jackal, the shrieking of a vulture, the wheeling of the kite and raven. He saw the hissing, guttering funeral pyres. Most terrible of all, he saw a female ghoul tearing apart a young woman's charred head.'

'The child was absolutely terrified. He fled from the place, screaming with fear and calling for his mother. As she came rushing towards him, he fell at her feet and died. His last words to her were, "Mother, look! Look! I gave my life to the demon that sits there within the funeral pyre in the cremation ground." '

"Oh what will I do now," said Gotamai, the mother, gathering her son's dead body in her arms. "What will I, a poor and lonely Brahman woman do now, left alone with my blind husband? Oh my son, who was it, demon or ghoul that ate up your life?"

'Holding her son to her breast, she went to the gate just outside the fortress wall and lamented loudly. "O Jambapati, guardian of this land," she called, "You who protect the dwelling places, the forests and water courses of this land, how is it that you deserted my son?" '

'And Jambapati did indeed come to her, her golden form gleaming. She said, "Who is it that calls out to me in sorrow, not minding this dark hour and the fearsome spirits that inhabit this place. What has troubled you?" '

'Gotamai said, "My innocent son, walking through this funeral ground was struck dead either by a demon or a ghoul. Look how he lies in my arms, as if asleep." '

'Jambapati said to her, "Neither demon nor ghoul was the cause of this boy's death, believe me; this is the just and appropriate end of his own past deeds and his own ignorance. So, Gotamai, cease your grief."'

'But Gotamai would not be consoled. Passionately she said, "Then gracious goddess, take my own life in exchange for his. Let him live to be a comfort to my blind husband."'

'Jambapati answered her with compassion. "Can you doubt that when the life-breath leaves the body, it must go along the appropriate path towards another birth that is the very result and consequence of its own past deeds? So, good woman, it is not possible· for me to bring back that life. Therefore, you must not grieve. As for my taking your life, that can never be possible; it would be like committing murder in the name of charity. And as for exchanging lives, are there not people always willing to give up their lives in place of the King? Yet in this very cremation ground there are thousands of memorials for kings who have died. So you must cease to think in this way."'

' " But the gods may grant boons, may they not? And if you, great goddess will not do this much for me, then I no longer care for my life," wept Gotamai.'

'Again the goddess told her, "Except for Mahabrahma, there is no deity in the lesser heavens who can grant a life." So saying, she summoned all the beings of the different worlds and of the several heavens that made up the entire cosmos or Chakkaravalam — the formless brahmas and those with form, the sun and the moon, the gods of great beauty, the assembly of stars — all indeed who were capable of granting boons. Then she said to them, "Listen to this woman's tragic tale and end her sorrow if you are able." Hearing all the gods confirm and repeat Jambapati's words, Gotamai at last overcame her distress, and accepting her son's death, she laid him gently upon the funeral pyre.'

110

The goddess Manimekalai Devi went on, 'This place is called Chakkaravala Kottam because all the gods of the entire cosmos gathered here to confirm Jambapati's message. Therefore the divine craftsman, Mayan, designed this place out of earthenware, as a replica of the cosmos, with Mount Meru in the centre, surrounded by the seven mountain ranges, the encircling oceans, and the four great islands.'

5

A Night of
Many Dreams

As Manimekalai Devi was telling this story, the two young women were overcome with weariness. They had reached the gate that the goddess had asked them to find. Slipping through, Sudhamati sank down and shut her eyes. Immediately the goddess gathered Manimekalai in her arms. Rising up into the heavens, she flew to a distance of thirty *yojanas* towards the south, to the island of Manipallavam. And there she laid down the sleeping girl.

The goddess still had work to do. She returned to Puhar and appeared to the prince Udayakumaran, who lay upon his bed, unable to sleep, waiting impatiently for dawn when he would continue his pursuit of Manimekalai. The goddess said to him, 'Son of Kings, if you, a Chola prince, act unrighteously, be sure that the rains will cease to fall and your people will die of drought and famine. Their lives should be your life. So give up your misplaced love for a woman who has chosen a life of renunciation.'

Next, she woke up Sudhamati from her deep sleep and said to her, 'Don't be afraid, Sudhamati, I am the Manimekalai Devi who came to attend the Indra festival in the city of Puhar. Knowing that the time is right for Manimekalai to begin her path towards the Buddha and his dharma, I have taken her away to the innocent island of Manipallavam. She will learn there of all her former lives, and return to this city in seven days. Even if she changes her form, she will never hide herself from you. Many wonderful things will happen in Puhar when she returns. And, Sudhamati, please also tell Madhavi that you have seen me. Tell her Manimekalai has now started on her quest for truth. Madhavi will remember that I appeared to her on the night that her child was given my name by Kovalan, for I am the goddess of his clan and protect the tall merchant-ships when they are upon the high seas. At dead of night I spoke to Madhavi in her dream and told her that she had borne a child of true piety, destined to release many from their sorrow and distress.'

Sudhamati sadly awoke and took shelter for the rest of the night at the great sanctuary, the Ulaga Aravi, in the middle of the Chakkaravala Kottam. Here, the Oracle of the Pillar, placed there by the divine craftsman, Mayan, spoke to her. He told her that in a previous life, there were three sisters, Tarai, Virai and Lakshmi, daughters of Ravivanman, King of Asodhara. She herself was once Virai, though in this life she was Sudhamati, only child of Kausikan, the Brahman of Sambai. Tarai was now Madhavi, and their youngest sister, Lakshmi, was now the Manimekalai they knew. This oracle also promised that in seven days' time they would all three be united once again.

At last, dawn broke. As the morning sounds of awakening birds and beasts filled the air, Sudhamati rose and sped along the wide streets of Puhar, anxious to reach Madhavi and to tell her all that had happened during the past eventful hours. The mother had been waiting, unable to sleep, her heart in her mouth. And after she had heard Sudhamati's words, the poet tells us, she was like a cobra that has lost its forehead jewel—a mere body uninhabited by life.

113

6
Manipallavam

But what of Manimekalai? She woke up on the endless white sands of Manipallavam, almost as if her life had fled elsewhere, seeking to be free of the ever encircling bonds of love. The sun rose slowly above the blue water. She recognised nothing about her. Could she still be in Uvavana, she asked herself. Then she called out, 'Sudhamati, where are you? Have you hidden yourself? Am I dreaming, or am I awake? Answer me, Sudhamati. It is daylight; Madhavi must be sick with worry. Oh, Sudhamati, have you forsaken me altogether? Could it be that it was not the goddess after all, but a strange woman who appeared to us at the crystal pavilion who has worked some trickery? Oh, goddess, you must help me now, for I am all alone.'

She rose to her feet. She wandered about the sand dunes which faced the waves of the sea like two opposing armies. The wide sea shore was deserted, except for the water birds. At some distance were laurel and screwpine trees, at her feet lay scattered shells, pearls and bits of coral that had been washed ashore. At last Manimekalai wept, thinking once more of Kovalan. 'Oh my father,' she mourned, 'you left Puhar for a distant land with the lovely Kannagi, and were cruelly put to death by the sword.'

Suddenly there appeared before her, a brightly shining shrine dedicated by the god of gods Indra himself to the Buddha, and bearing the dharma seat of the Enlightened One.

Transported by the sight, Manimekalai immediately raised both hands above her head in reverent salutation. The tears streamed from her eyes as she walked three times round the shrine from left to right, and then prostrated herself like a flash of lightning touching the ground. In that instant her previous lives were revealed to her.

'Oh sage Brahmadharma', she said, 'you truly had knowledge of what was to come. I see that all you said to me has come true. You were cousin to Attipati, King of Gandhara, and warned him of the earthquake which would swallow up his city and its surrounding land to a diameter of four hundred *yojanas*. The King sent his drummers and heralds throughout the land, warning his people of the coming disaster. Then all went northwards towards the city of Avanti. On their way they camped on the banks of the Kayankarai where you preached the comforting words of *dharma*. It was there that I came to you with my husband. I was then Lakshmi, the third daughter of Ravivanman and Amutapati; and I was married to prince Rahulan, born like a ray of light, the son of King Attipati and his Queen, Nilapati. On that occasion you said to me, "Prince Rahulan will die sixteen days from now, bitten by the snake Drishtivisha. You will enter the fire with him. You will be born next in the city of Kaveripuumpattinam or Puhar. There you will experience a great sorrow. At that time the goddess Manimekalai Devi will take you away and leave you on an island in the far south. You will see the *dharma* seat of the Buddha there, that bright place from where he spoke to the Naga kings, words that enabled them to open their ears to the *dharma* and close them to evil, banish anger from their hearts, and deliver themselves from the disease of rebirth. When you see the *dharma* seat, instantly you will remember your previous birth and recall these words that I speak to you now."

Manimekalai went on, 'When you finished speaking, I was heartbroken that my husband had to die so soon and I pleaded with you to tell me about my beloved Rahulan's future birth. You told me then that the goddess who took me away would reappear and speak to me about these things. Will she not come again, for I long to see her.'

At that very instant Manimekalai Devi descended to the earth, carrying flowers in her hands and saying to herself, 'Manimekalai has now understood her past lives from her vision of the shrine. And her own character is one of rare beauty.' To the young girl, she was like a ray of light descending into a dark and ignorant world. Recognising the goddess, she said, 'It is you who have come to me. I bow to your feet.'

First the goddess walked around the shrine and bowed to it. 'I praise you,' she said, 'both as the seat of the Buddha, and as the Enlightened One himself. I bow before you and I place you within my heart.' Then she turned to the waiting Manimekalai and spoke to her.

'Lakshmi, listen. There was once a time when you and your husband were in the palace gardens. You had just quarrelled; he touched your feet, anxious to win back you a favour. It was hot noon time. Just then the holy monk Sadhuchakkaran of the upper heavens came there, returning from Ratnadvipa where he had been preaching the Dharmachakkara. You were distressed and embarrassed to be found in such circumstances. Rahulan, on the other hand, was annoyed, and asked the monk angrily what he was doing there. You stopped his mouth with your hand and made him bow to the great one, saying, "Your mouth will be the poorer if you fail to show respect to the great sage." With that, you bowed to the disciple of the Buddha, and said to your heavenly visitor, "My lord, even though we are not your followers, allow us to bring you food and water. Please do us this honour." And the monk said to you, "Mother, I will be happy to eat what you give me." The good deed that you did that day will be the means by which you will end your cycle of birth'

'Now I must tell you that the prince Udayakumaran who followed you to the Uvavana gardens is none other than the same Rahulan, your husband in former births. Knowing that his love for you is unswerving, and that your heart too, cannot but be moved by him, I took you away, for I did not wish that the rare seed of dharma, which has been planted in you like a highly prized grain of rice, should melt away like a mere bead of salt.'

'Listen further, Lakshmi. Your two elder sisters, Virai and Tarai, married King Ducchayan from Kanga Nadu. At one time, as they were returning from the mountains, they came to the banks of the Ganga, where they met the great sage Aravana adigal. The sage said to them, "I came here to look for the mountain known as the Padapankaja, on which you can see the impression of the Buddha's feet. It is there that the Buddha, who set in motion the Wheel of Dharma, once stood long ago, as he preached to all living things. Out of his compassion he taught us how birth, death and all sorrow may cease, how even animals may get rid of the enmities and fears that lie within them and live at peace with themselves." Because they listened to Aravana adigal and worshipped there, they are with you today as Madhavi and Sudhamati.'

'Now that you have learned about your former birth and understood something about the four noble truths and the nature of *dharma*, it is important for you also to learn about all other religions and faiths, their doctrines and their attributes. But many teachers will refuse to give you instruction because you are very young, and above all, because you are a woman. So I will give you two mantras — one will enable you to change your form at will; and the other will enable you to travel the pathways of the skies.'

'Manimekalai, be certain that you too will attain the true *dharma* of the Buddha, who himself left aside the more common paths of knowledge in order to find truth and enlightenment on the auspicious full-moon day of *Vaikasi*. Now you may worship at the shrine once more and then return to your own land.'

The goddess rose high into the air and then suddenly descended once more. ' I forgot to give you one last mantra. Listen, dear child. This earthly body is made up of nothing other than handfuls of rice. Learn this mantra, and end the harsh pain of hunger.'

After the goddess had gone, Manimekalai walked alone among the white sand dunes, the water-springs and the strange wild flowers of Manipallavam.

She could see now the extraordinary beauty of the place, and its peace. She knew that it would soon be time to return to Puhar, but not quite yet. As she walked along, she was approached by yet another goddess, who came up to her and said, 'You seem to me like a young girl who has been the lone survivor of a shipwreck. Tell me, who are you?'

Manimekalai could not help smiling at the question.

'Beautiful one', she said, 'which of my individual births in the long stream of life do you ask about? In a past life, I was Lakshmi, wife of the great prince Rahulan. In this life I was born to the dancer, Madhavi ; my name now is Manimekalai. The goddess whose name I bear brought me to this island, and here, by the grace of the shrine to the sacred seat, I learned of my previous birth. This is my story. I have been greatly blessed here. And now, tell me who you are—you who are as lovely as a flower.'

The goddess was content then to speak to Manimekalai about herself. 'There is an island nearby, known as Ratnadvipa. A tall mountain in its midst, known as Samantamalai, bears on its peak the footsteps of the Buddha, who gave us the raft that can help us travel across the ocean of rebirth. I had gone to worship there. And there I accepted the guardianship of the shrine on this island upon the invitation of Indra, King of the gods. My name is Divatilakai.'

'Listen, Manimekalai,' she went on, 'it is only those who are true followers of the Buddha and his Dharma, who are granted the knowledge of their previous lives when they worship here. Such people are very rare, and have a special calling.'

'Now I have something more to say to you. There is a little lake in front of the shrine, covered with many water lilies. It is known as the Komugi lake. There, every year, on the full moon day of *Vaikasi,* the rare and famous alms-bowl known as Amudasurabi which once belonged to Aaputran, makes its appearance. Today is such a day. The time is now just right. I feel certain that it is meant to come into your hands. That bowl has a special quality. Any food that is placed in it—and all food is as precious as medicine to life—will always pass on into the hands of the needy ; it will never be empty. It is that paradox — a begging bowl that is also a source of abundance. You will learn of its history from Aravana adigal when you return to your own land.'

119

Manimekalai bowed once more to the blessed shrine and went with Divatilakai to the lake Komugi. They walked around it silently and waited with quiet hearts and minds. And the alms-bowl rose from the water, coming to rest in the hands of the steadfast girl. Overwhelmed with joy, she spoke out loud in praise of the Buddha:

> Conqueror of Mara, the Evil One.
> You who turned away from the hostile paths of wrong-doing,
> Who always strove to teach us the Dharma,
> Who renounced for yourself the bliss of nirvana,
> Who attained a knowledge far beyond most human thought,
> Who understood the truths that impart wisdom,
> Whose ears were closed to evil words,
> Whose tongue only spoke the truth,
> Who lived in order to release us from sorrow –
> I bow to your feet, for I have no other words to praise you.

Divatilakai then spoke to Manimekalai about the four noble truths, and told her about the evils of hunger. 'It destroys all things, family, fame, beauty and youth', she said. 'Worse still, it loosens our hold on the raft of learning. So I cannot speak highly enough of those who try and end hunger. Remember, to give in the hope of return is merely to trade, under the pretence of Dharma. True Dharma lies in doing the deed for its own sake. And in this wide world full of living creatures, to give food to the destitute is to give life. So in choosing to feed the hungry, you will be following a life of unblemished *dharma*.'

Manimekalai said, 'Just as a mother's breasts fill with milk when she looks with compassion upon her hungry baby, so this bowl will fill itself at the very sight of the poor, the homeless and the hungry. I long to see that.' Then, bowing before the feet of Divatilakai, and walking round the shrine once more, she rose into the air. True to the words of Manimekalai Devi, she returned to Puhar on the seventh day after she left it.

7
Manimekalai's Return

She came home for the last time to Madhavi who was sitting with Sudhamati, restless with worry, longing for her daughter's return, terribly afraid that something might have gone wrong, despite the reassuring words of the goddess. Like a miracle Manimekalai appeared before them and said, 'Eldest daughter of Ravivanman, and beloved wife of Ducchayan, I greet you. In my past birth my sisters Virai and Tarai, born of our mother, Amutapati, and in this life my own mother and dear friend, I touch your feet in honour and respect. The time has now come for us to put aside many things in our life together here. We must go now to Aravana adigal, to learn from him about the life of renunciation. This bowl that you see in my hands is the famed Amudasurabi which once belonged to Aaputran. Bow to it. And now, come, let us go to the sage,'

The three women arrived at the dwelling of the sage. He was expecting their arrival, and white haired and old though he was, spoke to them with wonderful clarity. Manimekalai bowed to him and told him of all that had happened to her from the time she entered the Uvavana garden with Sudhamati, until the moment when she received the four noble truths, and the bowl of Aaputran at the island of Manipallavam.

The sage said to them, 'People have forgotten about the path to *nirvana* which the Enlightened One taught us, or find it too hard to follow, so they are bound only upon the paths that lead to sorrow. Yet we are aware of the path to truth, just as we are of the sun, even when it is swallowed up by mist. We know it is there, even when we cannot see it clearly. So I continue my teaching, in the hope that the words of *dharma* may enter people's hearts and minds, little by little, drop by drop. The wide ocean may not enter the fine hole of a jewelled bead that is strung upon a narrow wire, yet a tiny drop may seep through.'

'At last a time will come when all the deities of Chakkaravalam will plead with the Buddha to descend from the Tushita heaven. And like the rays of the morning sun that dispels the darkness of the night, the light of the Buddha will shine clearly. All nature will be blessed and will bring forth abundantly, and men and animals will live together in peace, without fear or enmity.'

'But now, my child, there are several events which must run their

course in this city, events which will be brought about by your return here. It is only after that, that I may teach you all that I know. These two, your sisters in another life, will come with you on your final path, leaving behind all the bonds and attachments of this birth. Dear child, you have been granted this bowl, Amudasurabi, which is as medicine to life. Use it well, for to feed the hungry is a virtue to which both the gods and human beings aspire.'

As Manimekalai took into her hands the bowl which would be the means of ending for many the raging fire of their hunger, Aravana adigal told her its history.

8

Aaputran's Story

Once there lived in Varanasi, a Brahman, a teacher of the Vedas, by the name of Apanjikan. He had a wife, Sali. Now Sali had a secret lover. When she found that she was pregnant she feared the consequences, should her husband find out about it. She set off towards the south, claiming that she wished to bathe in the sacred waters of the Kumari. When her time came, at dead of night, she gave birth to a boy whom she abandoned in a distant garden, hardening her heart against him. And so she left.

Hearing the motherless baby crying out painfully from hunger, a cow that was passing by licked it with its tongue compassionately, gave it sweet milk, and took care of it for seven days, without once leaving its side.

Seven days passed by. Then a childless Brahman by the name of Bhuti came along that way, followed by his wife. Seeing the strange sight of the crying baby being comforted by a cow, Bhuti drew near and took up the child in his arms. 'You shall be my son, not the cow's', he said, shedding tears and thanking the gods, for he took the baby to be their gift.

They took the child home, rejoicing with all their relatives that their lineage would continue. Bhuti invested the child with the sacred thread as he grew up, and taught him, from his earliest childhood, all the scriptures that a Brahman should know. He came to be known as Aaputran.

When he was a young man, Aaputran one day entered the house of a Brahman of that town. There he found a cow, its horns covered with bright garlands, waiting to be sacrificed, sighing and lowing piteously. Its terror reminded him of a deer that has been trapped in a net and is waiting for the hunter's arrow. Aaputran was both shocked and moved to tears. Determined to prevent its death, he hid himself all day in the sacrificial hall, and at the dead of night he led the cow away and out of the city.

He was negotiating a difficult and stony path when the Brahmans caught up with him, accompanied by a great crowd of townspeople. They took hold of him and of the cow, and thrashing him mercilessly, demanded, 'What made you do such a wicked thing? You are unfit to be a Brahman, leave alone an ordinary human being.'

Meanwhile, the cow freed itself by using its horns to gore its tormentors, and fled away into the nearby forest. Aaputran, now asked mildly, 'Tell me, you learned Brahmans, what enmity is it that you bear against this cow which has only fed upon the grass from the common lands left for grazing by the King's orders, and which has yielded sweet milk and fed us with compassion since the days of our birth?'

123

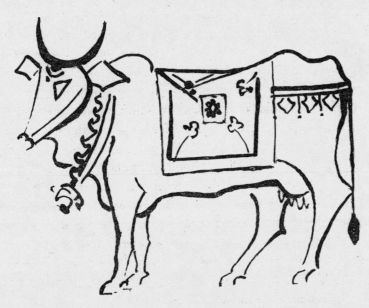

'Are you trying to ridicule us and the Vedas?' asked the men. 'You ignorant boy, you are only fit to be the son of a cow.'

'There are great sages whom you respect, who claimed descent from the cow, the deer, the tiger and the fox,' said Aaputran. 'Do the four Vedas declare anywhere that a lineage originating from a cow is degraded?'

Suddenly one of the older men gathered there, said, 'I know about the circumstances of this boy's birth. I have known it for a long time. I once met his mother, Sali, then emaciated from much travelling. She told me of the deserted field, one *kavatham's* distance from the Pandyan city of Korkai, where she abandoned her baby because he was not her husband's child. Because Bhuti told us where he had found the child, I knew instantly what his history was. I have been silent all this time thinking it would be profitless to repeat it. But we must shun him now. He is of low caste and will pollute us.'

Aaputran laughed. 'You who find it so easy to judge Sali,' he said, 'tell me, do you not know that the two great sages Vasishta and Agastya, progenitors of Brahmans, were born of a divine dancer and courtesan? Surely you cannot deny that?'

After that, even his foster father, Bhuti, was persuaded to close his doors to him, and so Aaputran went his way, alone, begging for his food. But the word spread that he was a cow-thief, and in all the towns and villages people jeered at him and threw stones into his begging bowl. So at last, he went south to the great and wealthy Pandya city of Madurai. Here he sought shelter at the entrance to the Sezhunkalai temple to the goddess Chinta Devi. In Madurai, he begged for food everyday at the houses of the rich. Then he called out to the blind, the deaf, the destitute and those who were suffering from disease, to share the food with him. He ate after everyone else had done, and at night he slept with the begging bowl for a pillow.

Now it happened once that at dead of night, when it was cold and wet, some travellers came to the sanctuary where Aaputran was fast asleep. Waking him up, they told him of their extreme, burning hunger. Aaputran, who could only give to others the food that he himself had begged, mourned his inability to feed these people. At that instant, within the temple, the light that is Chinta Devi herself began to burn brightly. And the goddess said, 'Do not be sorrowful. Rise up and receive this bowl. Even if the entire land should suffer from famine, this bowl will never be empty.' So saying, she placed the miraculous bowl into his outstretched hands. And Aaputran received it, praising her and singing aloud :

> 'Goddess who dwells in our inmost thoughts, Chinta Devi,
> Perpetual light of this Sezhunkalai temple,
> You who make my tongue to speak,
> First among the heavenly ones,
> Leader of all earthly beings,
> Put an end to the suffering that afflicts us all.'

124

So Aaputran appeased the hunger of his visitors of that hour, and from that day onwards, of all who came to him. And from that time, not only human beings, but animals and birds and all living creatures surrounded him, their sweet noise about him all the time, like that of birds that flock to a tree that is full of ripe fruit.

At last Indra, god of gods, came to hear of Aaputran's innumerable good deeds and charities. Disguised as an old man, bent of body, leaning on his staff, he appeared to Aaputran and said, 'I am Indra. I have come to you to reward you for your many charitable deeds.'

Aaputran laughed at this. 'King of heaven,' he said, 'you rule in a realm where there is neither giving nor receiving, where no one practises austerities or detachment. As for me, what possible reward can you give me that can equal the expression of tranquillity that I see on the faces of those whose unbearable hunger this bowl has appeased?'

Hundred-eyed Indra was angry with Aaputran for his contemptuous words. He made the rain to fall and the land to yield in great abundance. The kingdom of the Pandyas, which had for twelve years suffered drought and famine, became wealthy again. With the end of poverty, beggars ceased to come to Aaputran who was left without a vocation, and his bowl with no purpose. The little sanctuary where he had lived no longer resounded with the joyful noise of men and women feasting. People began to live wantonly, going about in their finery and wasting their time in gambling, lewdness and meaningless talk.

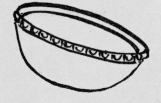

So Aaputran left that place where he had lived happily for many years and began wandering from town to town, seeking out those who were hungry and in need. But no one came to him. One day, he was walking along, like a merchant prince who was once very rich, but had lost his entire treasure at sea. Suddenly, some people, passengers of a ship that had just come ashore, came up to him and told him that the kingdom of Java was suffering from a great drought, and that many people were dying of hunger there.

Determined to go there and to be of use, Aaputran boarded the very same ship. No sooner had the ship sailed away than they were overtaken by a fearful storm. The captain lowered his sails and pulled in at Manipallavam. He said they must wait for at least a day. It grew darker; Aaputran climbed ashore and walked about the island. But that night, when the storm suddenly subsided, and the wind blew gently, the ship set sail once more. And in their haste, no one noticed that the new passenger they had taken on board had been left behind.

When he realised what had happened, the next morning, Aaputran was profoundly disappointed. He realised by then that Manipallavam was a deserted island. ' How can I bear to live here alone, using this bowl which is meant to feed multitudes,' he mourned. 'My vocation has now come to an end, for the meritorious deeds that brought it about are exhausted.' So he bowed in reverence to the bowl and surrendered it to the deep and clear waters of the lake Komugi. He bade it to appear again at that place once every year, and to enter into the hands of one who followed a life of discipline and compassion, and had undertaken to protect all living beings. Aaputran ended his life in prayer and fasting. Then, like the sun that appears in the eastern sky, dispelling darkness and ignorance, and in due course sinks to rest in the west, he left his body behind in Manipallavam.

Aravana adigal ended his story with these words. 'Let me finish the story, Manimekalai. Do you recall the good cow that fed and looked after Aaputran when he was abandoned at birth? It appeared to the sage Manmukan who lived by the Tavalai mountains in the green kingdom of Java. There, this miraculous cow with its golden hooves and horns never calved but gave its milk generously to feed the hungry. The sage, who knew all things past, present and to come, then predicted that the same cow would bear a son who would be a guardian and benefactor to all people, and that he would come out of a golden egg. And, just as he had predicted, Aaputran, who had never forgotten the cow that had protected him, was reborn on the same full moon night of *Vaikasi* that is sacred to the Buddha, in fulfillment of his dear wish to alleviate human suffering. The King of Java, Bhumichandran, hearing of the wonderful child, and himself being childless, accepted him as his own, given to him by the sage. And there he reigns today, wearing the garland of the king.'

9

Aadirai

'But let us think about Puhar,' said Aravana adigal. 'Whether it is because Indra is no longer being celebrated as before, or whether the Chola King's compassion towards his people has decreased, I do not know, but it is true that although the Kaveri flows full, and spreads over the land, the people of this country suffer from poverty and a lack of true well-being. Therefore, my child, to keep this wondrous bowl unused when it possesses the virture that could remove the suffering of this poverty-stricken land, would be as if the gods left one portion unused of the nectar that rose from the white waves of the milk ocean.'

Then Manimekalai rose and bowed to the feet of Aravana adigal, joined by Madhavi and Sudhamati who were as two mothers to her. Wearing the robes of a *bhikkuni*, she took the alms-bowl in her hand and went once again into the broad streets of Puhar. There the people recognised her as the beautiful woman whom the prince Udayakumaran had loved, and who had hidden herself away from his sight. They wondered that she now walked their streets so fearlessly and openly, begging bowl in hand. So they gathered about her, the Vidyadhara woman, Kayachandikai, among them.

Serenely Manimekalai looked about the street with its tall, well-appointed merchant mansions. Her heart filled with gladness that she was now about to begin her life's task. She said, 'Let me first receive into this bowl the alms that a good and virtuous woman alone can give out of the tenderness of her heart.'

'You stand at the very doorstep of such a one,' said Kayachandikai, who had been on her way southward from the *vidyadhara* city of Kanjanapura, and who had been cursed by a sage to suffer an unceasing and painful hunger. 'This is the house of Aadirai, and is Aadirai not the most generous and loving of women, the one lotus that outshines all others in its grace? This is the house that you must enter first.'

10
Aadirai's Story

And here is Aadirai's story as Kayachandikai told it; it recalls that of Kovalan and Kannagi, but it has a happier end. Aadirai's husband, Saduvan, like Kovalan, came of a wealthy merchant family. He too, neglected his young and innocent wife and went after the more exotic pleasures that were offered to him by a dancer. He spent his money lavishly on all kinds of gambling and dice games, until he had wasted away a large part of the family fortunes. The courtesan dismissed him when she found that he had no more money left, pointing out to him that there were other illustrious men whom she preferred. At last Saduvan realised to what a pass he had come. He began to travel, restlessly sailing abroad to trade and make good his losses. Then one day his merchant ship was caught in a violent storm and splintered in the high seas. Saduvan clinging to a piece of the wreckage, was washed ashore, to the mountainous land of the naked Nagas.

There were others who survived the shipwreck too, by hanging on to pieces of the strong mast of the ship. When they arrived home at Puhar, they reported that Saduvan, last seen fighting the waves in the middle of the ocean, had surely perished on that dark and terrible night.

When Aadirai heard the news, she wept aloud, and called to the people of Puhar to build her a funeral pyre in the cremation grounds. When it was lit, she entered it, determined to followed her husband into another life. But the flames would not touch her — neither her clothes nor the flowers in her hair, nor even the sandalwood paste she had spread upon her body. Aadirai was shocked. 'What sin have I committed that not even the flames will touch me! Oh, what shall I do now,' she mourned.

Then she heard a voice from the sky that said to her, 'Aadirai, listen. Your husband was carried away by the strong ocean waves to the mountainous land of the Nagas. But he will not stay there for very long. The merchant ship of one, Chandradattan, will come ashore there one day, and bring him home to Puhar. So, cease your mourning.'

When she heard this, Aadirai immediately emptied her mind of sorrow. She returned home, tranquil of heart, like one who has bathed in the clear waters of a lake. 'My beloved husband will come home soon,' she said, and took up her normal life of good works and charity with cheerfulness. And so she became loved and respected among all the women of Puhar.

Meanwhile, Saduvan, having suffered cruelly before he was finally washed ashore, fell into a profound sleep under a tree on the mountain-side. When he awoke, he found himself surrounded by the Nagas who were thought to be pitiless cannibals. They were now curious to find out how he had come there, all alone.

Now, it happened that because Saduvan had travelled so widely,

he had learnt the language of the Nagas, so he spoke to them in their own tongue. Astonished by this, they took him along to meet their chieftain. The chieftain was seated next to a woman, surrounded by pots of meat and drink, and looked like a bear with its mate.

Saduvan sat down in the shade of a nearby tree, and began to talk, winning over the Nagas by telling them of his adventures. The chief showed his sympathy and immediately offered hospitality, meat and drink, and told him to choose any of the young women there. To Saduvan, it was like a base parody of the life that he had once lived. He thought of the irony of it as he refused, vehemently. But the Naga chief was offended. Angrily he asked, 'What joy is there in this life, other than the pleasures of food, drink and women? If you know of

131

anything else, make it known to us.'

'Those who seek true knowledge do not drink because it confuses the mind, and they do not eat meat because to do so is to take life. Listen, friend. Those who are born in this world must die, and those who die must be reborn. Truly, it is like sleeping and waking. We have to avoid wrong-doing such as killing and drinking because we must all reap the results of our deeds.'

The chieftain was greatly amused. 'You just said that the life-breath that leaves the body takes a different form and enters a different place in another birth. Tell me, how is that possible?'

Saduvan said, 'Listen patiently, and do not be angry. When the body is inhabited by life-breath, it is open to sensations. But when life-breath has left it, the same body feels nothing, even if it is cast into flames. So we know that something has left the body. And it is not only I, but many others, who say that the life that has gone must find a place elsewhere. We all know, through the experience of dreams, that life-breath can leave the body behind and travel long distances. In a similar way, after death it can enter another body, an appropriate one that is the result of the life that has just passed.'

The Nagas listened, and asked Saduvan's help in finding a way of life which would be both virtuous and practical for them. In due course, when Chandradattan's ship arrived there one day, they heaped gifts upon him and sent him home. When Saduvan returned to Aadirai, he knew he was blessed beyond measure, and wanted nothing more than to spend the rest of his life virtuously and by her side.

Manimekalai heard Aadirai's story, and went up to the entrance of her house. She stood there, the poet tells us, as still and grave as an unembellished painting, her begging bowl held out a little. Aadirai came to her swiftly. She bowed to her, walked round her, and put food into the Amudasurabi, filling it abundantly. And as she did so, she said, 'In all this wide world, may the pain of hunger cease forever.'

132

The food that the virtuous Aadirai placed in the alms-bowl was what she normally cooked and served, and what she distributed to the poor everyday. But it increased many times, just as the merit that is the result of good deeds will always flow outwards, even more plentifully, in charitable deeds.

11

Kayachandikai

Now the *vidyadhara* woman, Kayachandikai, was suffering from a painful disease called *yaanaiti*, or elephant fire, which manifested itself in an unbearable hunger. She had followed Manimekalai closely. At last she spoke to her. 'Mother,' she said, 'I am cursed with a cruel hunger that is insatiable, a hunger that is like the ocean, prepared to swallow up even the mountain that was thrown into it when Rama and Hanuman's army tried to build a bridge across it. I beg you to cure me.'

Manimekalai took some rice from the bowl and put it into Kayachandikai's hands. That handful of rice immediately released the *vidyadhara* from her long hunger and distress. 'Mother,' she said, 'through you the curse that was laid upon me twelve years ago comes to an end today.' And overcome with gratitude, she told Manimekalai her story.

The land of the *vidyadharas*, Chedi, lies to the north, and is filled with silvery light. There in the splendid town of Kanjanapura was the home of Kayachandikai and her husband, Kanjanan. On one occasion, the two of them left their home, intent upon visiting the holy Mount Podiyil in the far south. As they went along their way, they found a tumbling mountain stream flowing into a pond filled with water lilies, its banks spread with sand. Enchanted with the place, they decided to bathe there.

A sage called Vricchigan came by, his sacred thread bright upon his chest and his hair matted into long, twisted locks. He was carrying, with great care, a *naaval* fruit, as big and shiny as if it were the fruit of a palmyra tree. Gently he placed it on a large leaf and stepped into the water.

The two *vidyadharas* came out of the river just then. Kayachandikai was curious about the object that the frightening old sage had left. Perhaps she was a trifle contemptuous too. Careless she was, undoubtedly. She nudged it with her toes. Then she rolled it under the ball of her foot.

At that moment, Vricchigan came out of the water, hungry, ready to eat. He hastened towards the fruit that he had left on the sandy bank.

Kayachandikai, startled, brought her foot down sharp. She had trampled upon the fruit!

Vricchingan looked at her sternly and said, 'That fruit possessed a miraculous quality. It came of a tree that yields a single fruit once in twelve years. Those who eat of that fruit will never suffer from hunger for another twelve years. As for me, I am under a vow to eat only once in twelve years. Today is the day that I break my fast. You have destroyed the food that I intended to eat.'

'Because of what you have done, you will lose the special *mantra* that enables a *vidyadhara* to fly through the air. And from this moment you will suffer from that dreaded disease called *yaanaiti* which will gnaw at your entrails unceasingly. On the same day, twelve years from now, that I eat the next *naaval* fruit that is ripe, your hunger too will end.'

After the sage had left, still in the throes of his hunger, the two *vidyadharas* were too shocked to pursue their journey to the famed mountain. Kanjanan had not liked what Kayachandikai did. Now he came up to her side and said, sorrowfully, 'I am afraid you are going to suffer pain because you hurt that austere man of divine powers. Come, let us rise into the air.'

It was at that point that she found that she could not utter the *mantra* that would lift her up. At the same moment a fiery hunger struck her, as if her very life would leave her dry, burning body. He, Kanjanan, hurried to fetch her fruit and vegetables. She would not, could not, be appeased. Hating to leave her, he spoke compassionately, 'In Jambudvipa, in the Tamil country, there is a famed city called Puhar. Many good people live there, who, because of the purity of their past deeds, are now able to befriend the needy and the suffering. It is best for you to go there, however long it might take.'

And that is what she did. Every year, when the joyous celebrations of the Indra festival took place, the *vidyadhara*, Kanjanan, would come to Puhar to see his wife and to mourn over her ceaseless hunger. And he counted the days that still remained before the curse would end.

Kayachandikai told Manimekalai all this. 'Because of you, my terrible hunger has come to an end. I salute you and bid you goodbye, for I am now free to return to my own land. But, Manimekalai, you must now go to the place known as Ulaga Aravi, or the great sanctuary of the world, which is always open to all people, and which is in the gardens of the Chakkaravala Kottam. Chakkaravala Kottam is where the monks who seek to end all suffering live; and the great sanctuary is where the hungry, the destitute and all who suffer from dire disease gather, looking for some deliverance.'

As Kayachandikai rose high into the air, Manimekalai went her way quietly and inconspicuously along the streets of Puhar until she reached Chakkaravala Kottam. Three times she walked round the Ulaga Aravi. She bowed to Jambapati, goddess and guardian of the place, and to the Oracle of the Pillar who knew all past lives and their consequences. Then she went to the poor and destitute who were gathered there, appearing to them, the poet says, like generous rain to a forest of trees that have withered dry. Holding out her bowl of food she said, 'This is Aaputran's Amudasurabi. Come, all you in need.'

12

Udayakumaran

For days together, ever since their astonishing absence from the Indra festival that year, Chitrapati had been nursing a grievance against Madhavi and Manimekalai. The message that Madhavi has sent her through Vasantamalai she found both incomprehensible and insulting. Now the news reached her that her grand daughter had returned to Puhar as a *bhikkuni* with an alms-bowl, and that she fed the poor everyday.

She felt such pain and anger when she heard this, it was as if a red-hot needle had been thrust into an open wound. She gathered her friends and kinswomen about her, all dancers, and spoke to them with great bitterness. 'When Madhavi grieved so much that her lover, Kovalan, had died, when she went to the sage Aravana adigal for instructions, and when she decided to take up a life of renunciation, I knew that she had made herself the laughing-stock of the people of this town. But what Manimekalai is doing now is even more ridiculous. Everybody knows this, above all the elders of this city, who know best what is appropriate and decorous. We do not belong to that class of women who dedicate their lives to one man, who pride themselves upon their chaste lives, and who take to the fire upon their husbands' deaths. Our role is different. We belong to no one. This is our right. Our lives are like musical instruments which continue to exist long after the bard has died and gone. Like bees, we must leave behind the flower that can no longer nourish us with honey. And like the Goddess of Fortune, we must abandon those men who have fallen upon evil days. But for one of us to wander about in the robes of a *bhikkuni* is the height of absurdity.'

'I tell you, my friends and sisters, I'll see that at least that pretty child, Madhavi's daughter, is handed over to prince Udayakumaran. He has been waiting for the opportunity all these days. I will myself pluck out the begging bowl from her hands, throw it at the beggars crowding about her, and hand her into Udayakumaran's chariot. If I don't succeed in this, I shall do the customary penance of our clan by walking around the dance stage carrying bricks on my head, and I will leave the house where my kinswomen and friends live honourably. I will go instead into the house of the common women who live by wrong-doing.'

Chitrapati sighed deeply as she said these words. Then, full of vengeance, she set off towards the prince's palace. When she arrived there, she found him in the audience hall where the pillars were decorated with coral, the walls laid with gold leaf and the entrance swept with fine sand. The prince himself was sitting on a throne hung with garlands, under a canopy sewn with pearls.

Chitrapati hailed the prince and said, 'The *kanchi* blossom, famed throughout this land of music and dance, is just ready to be picked. But you will find the flower in that base place, the Ulaga Aravi, where beggars gather, in the waste ground outside the renowned city of Puhar.'

He looked at Chitrapati with the expression of a man who has been shipwrecked in the high seas, and has suddenly found a raft. Then he told her how, several days ago, as he lay restlessly in bed, obsessed with the reflected image of Manimekalai that he had seen at the crystal pavilion in the Chakkaravala Kottam, a golden-skinned woman had appeared to him. 'I don't know whether she was a goddess or a miraculous vision,' he said, 'but she told me that as a righteous prince it is my duty to forget about Manimekalai, for she is bound upon the path of renunciation.'

Chitrapati laughed — it seemed — deferentially. 'Even the gods are known to have seen strange visions, particularly when they are drunk with love,' she said. 'So, royal prince, take no notice of what was said to you by someone unknown, in a dream. You must remember that Manimekalai was not born in such a family that she need stand guard over her virtue, first as a young girl, then as a wife, and then again as a widow, never letting her eyes look elsewhere, and worshipping her husband alone, to the exclusion of even the gods.'

'On the contrary, it is entirely right for her to display her skills in song and dance, to show off her beauty, to entangle men with her eyes and her words, to receive their gifts, and to leave them in due course, as a bee leaves the flower. It is equally right and fitting that you, a prince and the highest patron of arts, should subdue her.'

138

Too easily persuaded, Udayakumaran sprang into the chariot that waited for him with the horses already harnessed, and sped towards the great gathering place in the Chakkaravala Kottam. There she was, sure enough, begging bowl in hand, like a goddess in a wasteland, who feeds wild spirits that are possessed by hunger.

When he saw her, he was overcome by a curious pain. How could she have entered his heart so entirely, and then abandoned him to take up a life of austerities, a mere mendicant who begged for the food she ate? I have to ask her, he thought. He waited for a long time until she stood by herself, a little apart from the crowd. Then he went up to her and spoke his first words to her. 'Tell me, how is it that you have chosen this life of renunciation?'

Manimekalai felt a shiver run through her. She told herself that this was her husband of a previous birth, Rahulan, and that it was appropriate for her to show him respect; that she must answer him dispassionately even if her heart was moved by him, and even if he seized her hand as he did now. Quietly she withdrew her hand. She said, ' I will answer your question if you ask it sincerely, and if you truly wish to listen. I understood that this earthly life is a receptacle of sorrow, and that it is subject to birth, old age, disease and death. I wanted to lead a life dedicated to *dharma* and good deeds. As for you, you must do as you think right.'

Then she left the prince's side, and went inside where there was a shrine to Jambapati, guardian deity and ancestor. She bowed deeply to the goddess. Then, not being able to fathom Udayakumaran's mind, and thinking it best that he should not see her again in her own form, she spoke the mantra that Divatilakai had given her, changing her form to that of Kayachandikai. She thought she could do this safely, knowing that the *vidyadhara* woman had long left Puhar.

Udayakumaran, still standing where she had left him, aghast at her words, saw a figure whom he took to be the hungry beggar woman, Kayachandikai, emerge from the temple, an alms-bowl in her hand. No one else. He went into the presence of the goddess and said, 'I swear that I will find out where Manimekalai has hidden herself through some magic, after handing her alms-bowl to the wretched Kayachandikai. If you do not reveal to me where she is, I shall never leave you in peace. I touch your feet and make this vow; I swear I will take her away with me, for she has caught me as truly as the hunter entraps a wild elephant, as much with her wise and sweet words as by her beauty.'

A moment later, an attendant deity of the shrine opened its mouth and spoke to him. 'O prince,' she said, 'you have spoken too impetuously, and without thought. Your words to our goddess are

profitless; they can never come true. Understand this, and go your way in peace. It is useless to pursue Manimekalai.'

Udayakumaran was confused. What should he believe? First there was the vision of the golden-skinned woman who had told him to be steadfast in kingly virtues. Then he himself had seen what the miraculous bowl which Manimekalai held in her hands could do. Now here was this deity speaking to him directly and saying that his vow to the goddess was profitless. What should he do? For at the same time he continued to be deeply attracted to Manimekalai, and he could not believe that she was indifferent to him. 'I must watch her very closely,' he said to himself, 'for I have to know what she really feels.'

And so, at last, bowing to the goddess Jambapati, he went away. The skies had darkened and the crescent moon shone like a single ornament worn on the forehead of an elephant as Udayakumaran entered his palace.

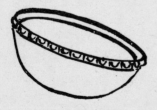

13

Manimekalai's Mission

Manimekalai now feared that were she to walk about the Ulaga Aravi in her true form, as Madhavi's daughter, the prince would never give her up. And so she decided to stay in the assumed form of Kayachandikai, who had become well known in Puhar as the beggar woman with the burning hunger. In this guise, in the following days, she went into the town, carrying her alms-bowl and feeding the hungry. At last one day, of her own wish, she entered the town prison where people who had committed all manner of crimes were held by the King. There too, she tended to the suffering.

Now the prison guards were astonished to see that she carried only a single alms-bowl, but fed so many. They decided to tell the King about this wonderful young woman and the bounty of her begging bowl.

The King was at that time in his gardens, walking about with his Queen, Seerthi. The flowers were in full bloom, the bees and dragonflies made music, the peacocks danced and the *koels* sang. A swan walked between two peacocks which were slowly twirling, their tails spread — like the sapphire blue Tirumal, the poet tells us, with his dark bride, Pinnai, dancing the Kuravai dance, with fair Balarama between them. Monkeys played about them and swung from the branches above them. Skilled dancers and musicians entertained them. And there were numerous attendants ready to string pearls, weave flower garlands, and adorn the royal couple with sandal paste and kumkum. Many wild animals such as the mongoose and rabbit and spotted deer roamed at will, delighting them; there were wells providing water for the plants, but also to form artificial lakes and ponds. There were hidden places and open pavilions. Walking past all these, the King and Queen entered their garden palace which had been fashioned for them by many skilled workers, jewellers from Magadha, goldsmiths from the Maratha country, blacksmiths from Avanti, and carpenters from the land of the Yavanas. The walls were overlaid with gold, the pillars were embellished with coral and had jewel encrusted capitals, and a fine canopy hung down, made of silk and sewn with pearls.

The palace guards allowed the prison soldiers to approach the King there. They stood respectfully at some distance, and praised him in the appropriate manner. 'May you live long, Mavan Killi, greatest of kings, you who have overcome the Chera and the Pandya with your great armies, and brought them low. Long may your white umbrella protect us. We have come to tell you of a strange thing. There has recently been a young woman in this city of Puhar, known to be suffering from the dreadful disease, *yaanaiti*. She was often to be seen, wandering about our streets and begging. But yesterday, she made her way into the prison, praised your name and fed the destitute who crowded about her. She fed all of them, and abundantly indeed, out of the single bowl she carried with her.'

The King was eager to meet the young woman, and asked for her to be brought to his presence immediately. When she came, he said, looking at her closely, ' I can see that you are a woman with a rare gift of piety. Who are you, and how do you come by that bowl?'

'Oh brightly garlanded King,' said Manimekalai, 'may you live long. May your land prosper. May the rains fall upon it in due season. May no evil harm you nor your people. Take me to be what you see — the daughter of a *vidyadhara*, forced to wander the streets of your beautiful city. This bowl was granted to me by a goddess. It has the virtue of appeasing even so insatiable a hunger as that caused by the *yaanaiti*. It has been as medicine to all lives suffering from the disease of hunger.'

'What must I do?', asked the King. 'Tell me and I will do it.'

'Free these prisoners,' said Manimekalai. 'Let it be a prison no longer. Let it be a place where people who have dedicated their lives to the dharma live.'

142

The King kept his word, freeing all prisoners that very day. Thereafter the former prison became a place where those people lived who only sought true wisdom and wished to do good deeds. By the command of the King who had accepted Manimekalai's plea, the prison house, cause of so much sorrow, became instead a place which contained a shrine to the Enlightened One who taught the four noble truths. It was surrounded by cells where the compassionate monks would dwell, and dining places where the hungry would gather.

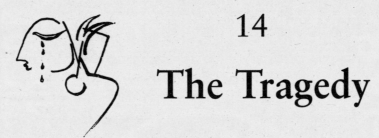

14

The Tragedy

Udyakumaran knew now that he was probably laying himself open both to the derision of the monks, and also to the wrath of the King, in pursuing a woman such as Manimekalai who had given herself to a life of renunciation. Then he came to hear of the strange woman's appearance before the King, his father, and of the King's gift to the monks. Once more he was filled with conflicting thoughts and wishes. Who was Kayachandikai? He determined upon one thing — that he would approach her in the great sanctuary, the Ulaga Aravi, where she was known to appear everyday, and ask her how she acquired her miraculous gifts, and whether she truly meant the words that she spoke.

It so happened that at the same time, there was someone else making his way to the same place. This was the young *vidyadhara*, Kanjanan, husband of Kayachandikai. He had counted the days and months and years since the dreadful curse spoken by Vricchigan, on the banks of the bounding mountain stream. That had been all of twelve years ago. The time had at last passed. The effect of the curse ought to have ceased. She should have returned home by now. Yet there was no sign of Kayachandikai, for whom he had been waiting so anxiously. At last he set off for Puhar himself, and began scouring the town square, and the flower gardens, the mansions and the monasteries and the public places. And so at last he came upon the strange sight of Kayachandikai dispensing food to the hungry people gathered in the Ulaga Aravi, and feeding them all out of her single begging bowl.

He was surprised and delighted at the same time. Joyfully he came up to her, and after many private words of greeting, which he supposed would be familiar only to the two of them, he said, 'I can see that although the bowl you hold in your hands is only a small one, it is able to appease the hunger of many. It must have been granted to you at last by the heavenly deities in order to end that fearful *yaanaiti*.' He spoke quietly, but also very confidently.

Manimekalai, busy about her work, had ears only for the clamour of the hungry. Kanjanan's words to her sounded not unlike those of everyone else who mistook her for Kayachandikai. It was true, she had meant them to do so. At the same time, it was never pleasant for her to confront the consequences of her own strategy.

At that moment she lifted her eyes and saw Udayakumaran slip into the Ulaga Aravi. She reminded herself firmly that it was in order to break his attachment that she had changed her form. Steadfast in that thought she went and stood next to him.

He had not expected this. He saw Kayachandikai. He heard the words of Manimekalai. She made him look about him at the old and aged who were gathered there. She pointed out to him that all things change, and that beauty and youth give way at last, inevitably, to ugliness, stench and deformity. 'Understand this truth about our living bodies, prince. It is a truth that we hide with flowers and scents and fine clothes and jewels', she said.

And what, meanwhile, of Kanjanan? What he saw outraged him. She paid no attention at all to my words, he said to himself, and willfully sought the company of someone else; she behaves as if she has no knowledge of me, and contrives to smile at the prince and to look into his eyes under the pretence of speaking words of wisdom to him. It is plain that he is her lover and that she has stayed on in Puhar only because of him. All his years of waiting, and this was the outcome. Bitter disappointment and jealousy filled him. He went inside the hall of assembly and hid himself in one of its shrines, the poet tells us, like a snake coiling itself into its pit.

Tragically, Manimekalai's words to the young prince Udayakumaran had a very different effect from the one that she had intended. He was suddenly convinced at what he had already guessed at — that the young woman speaking to him was actually Manimekalai, turned, through some magical skill known to her, into Kayachandikai's form. He had seen a young man, a foreigner, addressing her with familiarity just before she came up to him. Because of that man's presence there, Udayakumaran said to himself, she would not leave the Ulaga Aravi that night. He determined to return at a later hour, when it was dark, and find out at last what it was that Manimekalai intended.

At dead of night, when the city of Puhar was asleep, Udayakumaran left the palace all by himself, and slipping through its entrance, set off towards the great hall of assembly, the Ulaga Aravi. Quietly he climbed the steps up to the great hall, quietly he walked across it and towards Jambapati's shrine.

144

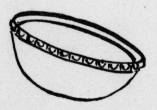

The scent of the sandal paste he wore on his chest betrayed him to the *vidyadhara*, sitting in the darkness of the hall, sleepless, his sword by his side. Kanjanan was now certain that Udayakumaran had come for Kayachandikai. With the speed of a cobra that rears its head and sinks its fangs into its enemy, he rose and flung his sword across Udayakumaran's neck. Seeing him fall, his head severed, Kanjanan had no thought except that he must find Kayachandikai and take her away with him, that instant, up into the skies.

Clear as a bell the voice of the Oracle of the Pillar, Kandir Paavai, placed there by the divine craftsman, rang out. 'Draw back, Kanjanan, *vidyadhara*, come no nearer. It is Manimekalai whom you saw here, wearing the form of Kayachandikai. I will now tell you what happened to your wife after she was cured of her dreadful disease.

'You know that those who are privileged to travel through the skies must never fly across the Vindhya mountains, sacred to the goddess Durga. They know that anyone who dared to do so will be caught by the shadow of the guardian spirit of the mountains and be drawn into its belly. That was the tragic fate that befell Kayachandikai, too anxious, too hasty in her return home.

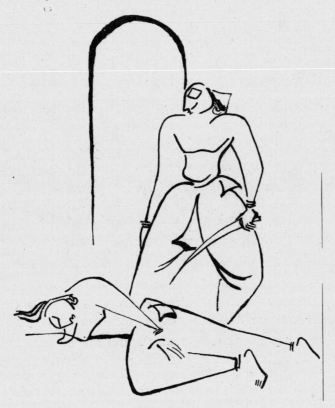

'And now listen carefully to what I must tell you. Although Udayakumaran's death in so horrific a manner is the result of his own past deeds, this, your violent action done out of senseless anger and thoughtlessness must follow you all your life.'

Realising only too well the enormity of what the oracle said, and of what he himself had done, Kanjanan rose with his burden of sorrow and went his way to his own land.

Manimekalai, asleep within the shrine to Jambapati, woke to hear the words of the Oracle of the Pillar. At once she understood the full horror of what had happened. 'Let me be rid of this form,' she thought, 'alas, how little it has helped me.'

Herself once more, and weeping bitterly, she addressed the body of Udayakumaran : 'A long time ago, in our former life, when the poisonous snake Dhrishtivisha struck you down, I was ready to give up my own life on the funeral pyre. Even as recently as in the Uvavana gardens, my heart was still drawn towards you. Because of that the goddess Manimekalai took me away to the island of Manipallavam and granted me the vision of the seat of the Buddha, of him who broke free from all bonds of attachment. There, in the presence of the shrine, I understood my former birth and the whole course and stream of my being. Alas, dear one, I took on the form of Kayachandikai only to tell you these things. I wanted to tell you that all who are born must die, and all who die must in their turn find their next birth. I wanted to tell you of the sorrow that is the result of evil deeds, and of the peace we achieve by doing good. I wanted to tell you these things only that your life should be free of evil and its consequences. But alas, you fell to the cruel sword of Kanjanan.'

Once again the Oracle of the Pillar, the deity of Ulaga Aravi, spoke out sharp and clear: 'Do not go near him; do not touch him. Let him be. It is not merely in one life, but in many, many, long gone, that you were this man's beloved wife, and he was your dear husband. But you who seek to leave this cycle of birth which is so full of confusion, change and instability, must now cease this. Cease to mourn him.'

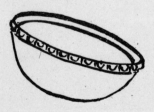

146

Manimekalai bowed to the deity. 'Are you the oracle of this place, the golden god of the Pillar who speaks only the truth? I touch your feet and ask you this. Tell me why in a previous birth his life ended because of a vicious snake, and why he lost it now because of Kanjanan's sword of anger. By your grace I only want to hear and understand.'

The oracle said to her, 'When you two, Rahulan and yourself, came to the banks of the river Kayankarai to hear Brahmadharman the monk preach the healing words of the Buddha and of his return, you also asked to be granted the privilege of feeding the sage the next morning. And indeed he agreed, and the two of you left his presence joyfully. On the next day, one of the cooks arrived late to work, and already nervous, anxious about getting the meal ready in time, the cook somehow tipped over the great vessel that held the rice. Rahulan who should have known better, for he had been taught the five *silas*, was so overcome with anger at this sight that he drew his sword and severed the man's head from his shoulders. It is this evil deed that has not yet left him. Nothing and no one can prevent us from living through the consequences of the evil that we do, and it can follow us through many lives.'

147

'Let me tell you something else, Manimekalai. My name is Tuvatikan, and I belong to the great group of heavenly beings. I do not ever leave the image that Mayan, the divine carpenter made for me and placed within this ancient pillar. Yet I know all events past and to come.'

After this, on Manimekalai's request, the oracle told her of the many events that were yet to come in the long life ahead of her, and in her future lives in Uttara Magadha, until at last she was destined to be one of the chief disciples of the Buddha. Tuvatikan told her, too, that Manimekalai Devi had known all this when she appeared in the Uvavana gardens and took her away to Manipallavam.

Manimekalai listened to all that she was told and thought about it. At last she felt a great peace, as if she had at long last struggled to the shores of the ocean of sorrow. Her mind had freed itself of its distress, the poet tells us, like a peacock shaking itself free of a binding net. And at once the sun rose, putting to an end the darkness of the long, long night.

15
Aftermath

Already at sunrise, news had spread throughout Chakkaravalam, amongst the ascetics living there, of the terrible death of the prince during the night. They came in a body to question Manimekalai. She spoke to them without trembling, telling them all she knew. The monks listened to her words and believed her. Then they left her and the dead prince in a hidden place and went to seek the King's presence.

They announced themselves to the gatekeepers of the Chola palace, and were ushered into the presence of the King, Mavan Killi. They greeted him saying, 'May your white umbrella, like the full moon in the highest heaven, give cool shade to your people. May your spear and your sceptre be always compassionate. May the discus you hold in your hand roll without evil intent. May you live happily throughout the years that are allotted to you.'

Then, one of the most distinguished of that assembly of sages stepped forward and spoke for the rest. 'O King,' he said, 'You who rule the earth know that not only in these times, but in former days too many men have lost their lives because their own bad deeds came to fruition. Some in their lustfulness have pursued virtuous women. Others have even set their hearts upon women who are known to have renounced the world.' The learned one then told the King the story of Kagantan and his two sons.

The virgin goddess Jambapati once appeared to King Kantan and said, 'Leave this city, for Parasuraman is under an oath to split apart all kingly lineages, and it would never be possible for you to take arms against him.'

Kantan decided to do as the goddess bade him, but he thought carefully about whom he should ask to rule in his place. He called to mind Kagantan, the son of his mistress, a dancer. This Kagantan was known for his courage throughout the island of Navalam or Jambudvipa, and he never made a mistake even when his enemies raged against him.

Now Kantan sent for him and spoke to him affectionately. 'Parasuraman will certainly not harm you, for he will not consider that you are directly of the kingly lineage. So, Kagantan, protect this city and be its guardian until such a time that the sage Agastya can put an end to my distress, and recall me here with his gracious words.' Renaming the city Kaganti in honour of its new protector, the King slipped away in disguise, that very night.

Soon after this, one day, Kagantan's younger son was strolling by the mouth of the river Kaveri. He saw a young Brahman woman, Maruti, returning from a bath in the clear river waters. Because she was alone, he instantly assumed that she was an immoral woman, and he called out to her suggestively, 'Come here to me.'

Maruti was deeply distressed by this and said to herself as she hastened in the direction of her home, 'If women are truly chaste and are able to call down the rains to fall upon the thirsty land, they will never enter the hearts of men other than their husbands. But I seem to have done this dreadful thing. So I am not fit any more to guard the three holy fires of my husband who wears the sacred thread upon his chest.'

So saying, full of confusion, Maruti walked past her house, and on towards the crossroads where the famous *bhutam* of Puhar lived. There, she pleaded, 'From the time I entered my house as a little girl, I have never once failed my husband. Yet it was easy for this man who merely looked at me, to hide me in his heart. I took on the duties of a virtuous woman who may even summon rain; I am not conscious of any misdeeds that I might have done. You are the god of the crossroads who swallows up wrong-doers. Judge me now, for has your justice been ever known to fail?'

The great *bhutam* of the crossroads appeared to her then and said, 'Listen to me, Maruti. You did not understand clearly the words of the ever-truthful Valluvar when he said, "Rain falls when it is summoned by a woman who worships her husband alone when she wakes, before she worships any other god." You listened to the false words and frivolous talk of others, and became involved more in rituals and in the celebration of festivals. Because of this, you may not call down the rains, nor burn out the hearts of lustful men. But of course, it is possible to mend your ways, and because you are not one of those women who act as they please, my cruel noose will not bind you.'

'As for that young man who has remained unrepentantly lustful, I cannot punish him unless the king fails in his duty to bring him to justice within seven days. However, it will surely happen that King Kagantan will hear of this incident before that, and cut him down with his sword.' And so indeed, ended, the life of Kagantan's second son.

Now at that time, there lived in Puhar, a man called Dharmadattan. In the same street there lived his mother's brother's daughter, Visakai of the beautiful dark eyes. They were both outstandingly good-looking, like celestial paintings made by the gods and cherished by them. Because of this, and because they were cousins, who could marry each other, an evil canard had spread in the city that Visakai had consented to a *gandharva* marriage with Dharmadattan.

When this came to her ears, bright-browed Visakai left her home in haste, not even adorning herself. She went straight to the Ulaga Aravi, and addressing the brightly shining image there, she said, 'I beg you to end this slander against me and to clear my name.' At once the speaking image called out in a loud voice and addressed the people of Puhar: 'I testify to the chastity of this woman; she is one of the pure of heart who can call down the rains.'

Visakai knew perfectly well that the people of that town would never have freed their minds of her supposed moral flaw, had not the goddess cleared her name. So she vowed, 'I will only be my cousin's wife in another birth. In this life I will never unite with him.' And after speaking to her mother at length about the attributes of a good life, she entered a house for women renouncers.

After this, Dharmadattan praised the speaking image for removing the distress that had overcome them all. Then, taking his mother and father with him, he left the great city of Puhar and went to southern Madurai which teemed with many wealthy and illustrious people.

Dharmadattan too, made a vow. He said he would never wish for a woman other than his uncle's daughter, Visakai of the flower-adorned hair. Therefore he would wait patiently for this birth to pass away.

150

So time passed. Dharmadattan became one of the leading men of Madurai, famed as much for his wealth as for the righteous means by which he had earned it. And when he attained the age of sixty, the King honoured him by conferring upon him the emblem of the *etti* flower.

But on that important occasion, a Brahman came to him and said, 'Consider, Dharmadattan, what exactly have you accomplished here, in Madurai? Do you not know, however many good works you perform, as a man without a virtuous wife by your side, you will never enter the world of celestial beings? If you understand what I say, then it is time for you to return to your own city.'

Hearing this, Dharmadattan left southern Madurai, and once again returned to Puhar, hopeful that after all these years, he might marry Visakai.

When Visakai of the golden bangles came to hear of Dharmadattan's return, she came out of her house boldly and met him without a trace of shyness. Going up to that man who had led a blameless life, she looked directly at him and said, 'Dharmadattan, you and I can scarcely recognise each other. Admit this to yourself. Answer me: where has that beauty fled away, for which we were so well known when we were young? You are now sixty years old. Look at my hair, see how the grey spreads through my five braids. Youth and desire, where have they gone? No, in this life, I can never be your wife, but in our next birth I will be happy to serve you.

151

'Neither youth nor this earthly body can remain constant. Wealth, however abundant and however excellently won, cannot remain constant. Believe me, neither spouse nor children can help us to attain the celestial worlds. The discipline of good deeds alone can help us to that end. Therefore, Dharmadattan, give charitable gifts.'

Dharmadattan listened to her, and together they planned many good deeds in Puhar, exceeding in number even the stars in the wide skies. And Visakai lived and died a virgin, who never married.

Now this same Visakai, a long time ago, soon after the speaking image had cleared her name, was one day walking down a street strung with banners. Kagantan's eldest son, whose younger brother had been punished because of Maruti, saw her there. His heart darkened and hardened with lust. He pursued her and schemed to win her. The young man had intended to remove the bright garland that he wore encircling his curly dark hair and to place it on Visakai's, claiming that this was an ancient form of marriage, and he might therefore possess her. But when he raised his hand to touch his hair, he could not bring down the garland.

When Kagantan came to hear of his eldest son's evil intention and its terrible consequence, bitter anger and pain twisted his heart. Yet forgetting his pain, he cut down his own son with the sword.

The sage ended the story of the two sons of Kagantan, and said, 'May you live long, King of kings, and protect this land from age to age.'

The King knew that the learned one had more to say. 'You began with the words "not only in this day", and went on to speak of many moral lessons. Tell me then, has such an evil deed happened today?'

'May your sceptre always be free from evil,' said the sage. 'Oh King, the sages who seek true knowledge tell us that there are five evils that are forbidden throughout the sea-girded world. Of these, lust causes all the other four: intoxication, falsehood, theft and murder. Those who cast away lust from their hearts cast away all other evils. Only those who are truly without desire can become ascetics.'

The sage went on, 'You have perhaps heard that Madhavi, after the tragic death of her lover, Kovalan, gave up the life of a dancer and went to a monastery to listen to the good counsel of the monks. Her daughter, Manimekalai, even though so young, took up a life of renunciation, begging for alms in small and large houses, and living in the great sanctuary.

'Your son, Udayakumaran shadowed her many days, even though he knew perfectly well that Manimekalai had chosen such a life. He could not rid his heart of its lust. Even after she had changed her form into that of a *vidyadhara* woman, Kayachandikai, he followed her, boldly entering the temple at dead of night. Now, because Kayachandikai had actually been in Puhar not so long ago, her husband came here in search of her. When he found Udayakumaran entering the temple, he assumed that he had an assignation with his wife and cut him down with his sharp sword. All this happened because Udayakumaran's own evil deeds came to a due end.'

152

When the Chola King, Mavan Killi heard the sage's account, he was filled with sorrow. Yet he composed himself and said, turning to the commander of the Chola army, 'What the *vidyadhara* did was not right. But only in that he brought the prince to justice while it was my duty to do so. One thing is certain: without the protection of the King there can be neither chastity among women nor true penance among ascetics. Let Udayakumaran's body be placed upon the funeral pyre immediately. I want the young woman, the daughter of Madhavi, put under guard.'

16

Manimekalai and the Chola Queen

It was Seerthi, the Queen, who was totally overwhelmed with grief. The Chola King immediately sent for an old woman, Vasantavai, in order to speak wise words to Seerthi, and to comfort her. This woman stayed for many hours, speaking of Udayakumaran's life and the manner of his death, and at last, she left. The Queen hid her sorrow and anger deep in her heart. Secretly she was determined to take revenge on Manimekalai, whom she blamed for her son's untimely death. But outwardly she seemed calm. A few days later, she came up to the King and greeted him. 'Righteous King,' she said, 'I have thought long about this terrible thing that happened to my son. Yes, Udayakumaran was not fit to rule this land; it was a great wrong on his part to pursue one who had renounced the world and taken up the robes of a *bhikkuni*. But equally, it is not right for us to imprison this woman who has renounced both love and youth in the name of her quest for truth.'

'You now know that only those who are truly virtuous can be called the sons of kings,' said the King sadly. 'You may release Manimekalai if that is your wish.'

Seerthi immediately went and brought away the young woman, saying, 'Come and stay with me for some time. No one will prevent you from begging for alms.'

Now the Queen's plan was first to drug Manimekalai until her mind was gone, and then to put her out into the streets so that the outraged people of Puhar would hit her with sticks and stones and turn her out of town. But Manimekalai already had foreknowledge of her future, and remained in full possession of her senses, despite the evil medicine the Queen gave her.

Seerthi was frustrated and enraged. She then sent for a wild and ignorant youth, and bribed him with much gold. She told him to

molest the girl and then spread the slander that Manimekalai had
seduced him. The reckless youth agreed to do as he was asked, and
went into the Queen's inner rooms by a secret corridor. But once
again, Manimekalai had foreknowledge of the Queen's intention.
This time she spoke the *mantra* that the goddess had given her on the
island, changing her form into that of a man. The youth who had
been so easily bribed was shocked when he saw a young man in the
Queen's rooms. He knew that no man could enter there without
royal permission; even the guards were women. 'I don't know what
evil intention is in this wicked Queen's mind,' he thought. And he
fled from the palace and left the town that very night.

But Queen Seerthi would still not give up. 'Why should this
woman be spared her life, when my only son had to die for love of
her,' she asked herself. So she dragged Manimekalai into a dungeon

and locked her up there without food or drink, giving out that Manimekalai was suffering from a mortal disease and refusing food. Days passed, however, and Manimekalai, who had the means to prevent hunger, remained cheerful, showing no signs of failing health.

At last Seerthi realised what she had been doing. She came to Manimekalai and begged her forgiveness. 'Be patient with me, you who are like Lakshmi,' she said, 'I was so overcome with sorrow when my son died, I did not know what I was doing.'

Manimekalai spoke in her turn, and said to her: 'In another life, Prince Rahulan, son of Nilapati, died of the vicious poison of the snake Drishtivisha. Where were you then, what were you doing, while I was ready to give up my life in the fire for grief of him? Consider carefully, Queen, and tell me this. Are you grieving now for your son's body, or for his life-breath? If you mourn for his body, remember who it was who laid it upon the fire. If you mourn for his life, remember that you cannot know where it is now; where the result of his past deeds have taken him. So, if you once loved your son, you can only give your love and compassion to all living things equally.'

Then Manimekalai told the Queen what she had learnt of Rahulan's previous life through the words of the oracle in the great sanctuary of Ulaga Aravi. 'I had foreknowledge of all that you planned to do against me,' she added, 'but I never wished to leave this place or to go away before healing your sorrow. For you are the mother of one who, in a former life, was my beloved husband. I wanted to tell you of the five evils of desire, intoxication, falsehood, theft and murder which bring sorrow into our lives. I wanted you to understand that only those who have finally rid themselves of the anger in their hearts can attain knowledge; that only those who give to the suffering poor can be said to live in this wide world; that only those who feed the hungry are fit to enter the celestial world, and only those who love all living beings can reach beyond sorrow to truth.'

In this way, Manimekalai sprinkled the Queen with the waters of wisdom, and so at last quenched the sorrow which had raged like a fire in her heart. Seerthi's mind suddenly became clear and she bowed to the young girl with respect. But Manimekalai, in her turn, touched the older woman's feet saying, 'It is I who should bow to you, for you are the mother of one who was once my dear husband, and what is more you are the Queen of this great land.'

17

Manimekalai Leaves Puhar

Chitrapati knew that she was the one who had goaded Udayakumaran to go in search of Manimekalai at midnight. Now she was struck with fear and horror when she heard that the prince had been cut down by the *vidyadhara's* sword. Her one overpowering anxiety was to rescue her granddaughter from prison. Hastening to the palace, she fell at the Queen's feet.

'Greatest of queens,' she said, 'there have been many famous dancers in this proud city. I myself can recite to you the stories of at least one hundred and twenty one of them. But I assure you not one of them suffered the sorrow that I suffer today. I beg you to let me take Manimekalai away with me. It has become a matter of scandal and ridicule in this town that first Madhavi took religious instruction from Aravana adigal, and now, what is far worse, Manimekalai has been seen begging for alms from door to door. She is a girl who was brought up to perform upon the stage. The people of Puhar know that her present behaviour is not suitable to women of my profession. So please tell her she must come home.

'Besides this, O great Queen, I am filled with foreboding that terrible harm might yet come upon this city, even more dreadful than this tragic death of our prince. Let me remind you of our recent history.

'When our King Nedumudi Killi was sitting among the palm trees one spring day, not very long ago, watching the play of the waves upon the shore, a young woman appeared before him. The King was quite overcome by her beauty, as if Kama's flowery arrows had assailed all his senses. He who had been victorious over so many enemies, and now well past his youth, was lost to her completely. As for the young woman, she stayed with him for a month and then disappeared without a trace, never once telling him who she was.

'We know that the King was devastated by her disappearance and searched for her everywhere. At last he came to a sage who had acquired special powers and could live in either water or land, and could even fly in the air. The Chola bowed before him and said, "She who is as dear to me as my own life has left me and vanished away. Tell me, O sage, have you seen her anywhere?"

'The sage replied, "I have not seen her, but I do know of her. She is Pilivalai, the daughter of Valaivanan, renowned ruler of the Nagas; his Queen is Vaasamayilai. On the very day that the girl was born, the astrologers predicted that as a young woman she would bear a King's child. I tell you that her son will return to you one day, but she, never. Therefore, do not look for her any more. There is, however, something that it is my duty to warn you about. Listen carefully. The day you forget to hold the Indra festival, this great city that is entrusted to your care will enter the womb of the sea. The goddess, Manimekalai Devi herself has sworn to this, and Indra has added his oath. So, King, be on your guard."

'Since that day, the people of this city have never been free of fear lest Manimekalai Devi should be displeased. Great Queen, I am terrified that the goddess will surely take revenge if the young girl who bears her name should come to any harm. So please let me take her away with me.'

However, the Queen was adamant in what she said. 'Your profession, Chitrapati, is founded on those same five things that the truly enlightened seek to remove from their lives — intoxication, lies, lust, and dark thoughts of theft and murder. Please accept that Manimekalai has renounced that life. She will never re-enter your house. Rather, she will stay with me here.'

Meanwhile, Madhavi, too had heard of Manimekalai's predicament. Once again she was in danger of losing her hard won peace of mind. Once again she spoke to Sudhamati of her troubled heart. Together they went to Aravana adigal, bowed at his feet, and brought him to the Queen's presence.

The Queen rose immediately and bowed to the sage, joined by Manimekalai, Chitrapati and all the attendant women present. He blessed them with the words, 'May you attain true knowledge.'

With great respect the Queen led him to a seat that was set aside for monks and revered visitors such as he. Then, having done him all the honours that were due to him, she asked him what good deeds she herself might have done to merit his visit.

'Good queen,' said Aravana adigal, 'my life, like the sun speeding to the west, is nearing its end. But it is natural that all who are born must grow old and ill and die at last. I come to bring you the words of the Buddha.

'The Buddha has taught us that our lives are bound upon a wheel of causes and effects, beginning with ignorance and ending with rebirth. Those who understand this will gain true rewards; but those who do not, condemn themselves to suffering.

'My friends, if you should ask what is ignorance, I will answer this: it is the refusal to understand these twelve links of causes and effects; to be deluded into believing that what is false is true.

'The universe of sentient being is endless, and there are six types of living beings upon it: human beings, gods with form, gods of the lower heavens, demons, beasts and ghosts. We are each born to be

one of these, depending upon our deeds. For the total result and effect of a past life must enter the seed of each new living being, bringing either happiness or sorrow.

158

'My friends, what is evil? It is to give in to three kinds of action — murder, theft and lust; to indulge in four kinds of speech — lies, slander, harsh or useless talk; to allow desire, anger and delusion to sway the mind.

'What then is good? It is to be free of these ten evils; it is to practise the rules of morality; it is always to be charitable.

'Good Queen, may you and your women walk in the paths of *dharma*. As for you, my child Manimekalai, you still have a task ahead. You must go now and learn all that you can about the doctrines and disciplines of all known religions. When you have done that, it will be time for me to give you my last words.' So saying, the sage rose to his feet, ready to leave.

Manimekalai went up to him at once and touched his feet. Then she too addressed the Queen and all the women gathered about her — Chitrapati, Madhavi, Sudhamati and the attendant women. 'Do as the sage has told you', she said. 'Never forget his words. As for me, if I continue to stay here in this city, people will always say that I was the cause of the prince's death. So let me leave now, first to seek Aaputran; then to Manipallavam, that island of peace, and then onward to the great city of Vanji where I shall seek the shrine of Kannagi. Please do not fear that any harm will come to me.'

It was sunset time, the sun's rays were like molten gold, gradually cooling. Manimekalai went to the Ulaga Aravi to pay her respects to the goddess Jambapati and to the shining oracle. Then she went round the temple, and at last she rose high into the air.

She alighted in a garden laid out on the outskirts of the capital city in the island of Java. There she rested until day break. At dawn she sought out the sage Dharmasavagan who lived in those gardens. She asked him where she was, and who was the ruler there.

'This is Nagapuram, capital city of Java', said the sage. 'The King who rules over us is Puniyarajan, son of Bhumichandran. From the day that he was born, we in this city have never known drought. The land is fertile, the trees and plants yield abundantly, and the people know no illness nor disease.'

18

Puniyarajan's Pilgrimage

The sun rose higher in the sky. That morning the King and his court came to pay their respects to the sage Dharmasavagan, and to listen to his wise words about the different paths of good and evil; about that which is impermanent and that which is lasting; about the nature of sorrow; about the journey of the life-breath; about the twelve interdependent links in the chain of causes and how to be free of them; and about that profound peace that is at the centre of the Buddha's word.

Then, the King noticed the new-comer in their midst. 'Who is this striking woman who seems to have renounced the world at so young an age, and stands here, begging bowl in hand?' he asked.

The chief minister who stood at his side answered him. 'There is no one who can be compared to this woman in the entire island of Java. You will remember that sometime ago I sailed to Kaveripuumpattinam on an embassy from you to the Chola Killivalavan. In that city I met the sage Aravana adigal who spoke to me about this very young woman. I remember reporting to you, as soon as I returned about her and her good deeds. And now here she is, herself.'

At that instant, Manimekalai stepped forward. 'O King, this alms-bowl that I am privileged to hold is the very same that was once in your hands.'

She saw the look of amazement and incomprehension on the King's face. 'Alas', she said, 'you have forgotten this, you who are now a great King. But even though you may not be aware of your past life, you must surely know of your present one, and how you were born of a cow?'

Puniyarajan was speechless at her words. Manimekalai spoke again. 'I see that you must go to the island of Manipallavam with me and worship at the shrine of the Buddha there. Then alone will you understand fully the cycle of birth and its attachments. We shall meet there, O King.'

Manimekalai rose once more into the pure regions of the air. Before the sun had set, she climbed down from the sky on to the shores of Manipallavam where the ocean waves lapped endlessly and the air was full of the scent of flowers. She walked along the shores of the island with the great inward peace of one who has come home. Once again she was granted the vision of the shrine, and saw into her past lives. The words of Brahmadharman, spoken so long ago on the shores of the Kayankarai returned to her once again. As if they had been spoken to her yesterday, with the same clarity, the words came back to her, telling her of the wisdom of the Buddha who knew that all things were impermanent; predicting Rahulan's death; describing this very sacred seat which had been made long ago by god Indra and which would make her past lives known to her.

King Puniyarajan, meanwhile, had taken Manimekalai's words to heart. He left the garden and set off home to his palace. There, he went immediately to the apartments of Amudasundari, the old Queen, whom he had always assumed to be his mother. He asked her about the true circumstances of his birth. So at last he came to know how he had come out of the golden egg which had been carried by the generous cow of the sage Manmukan, and how the same sage had given him away to the childless King.

When he understood all this, Puniyarajan was overcome with sad thoughts about the nature of this life. Those things that had always been a means of joy to him — music, dance, the love of women — no longer seemed pleasing in the same way. 'Perhaps I too should follow the path of renunciation,' he said to himself. 'The seeds of wisdom that Dharmasavagan has taken pains to plant in me have been watered today by Manimekalai. At last they begin to sprout.'

The chief minister, Janamitran, was immediately aware of the King's change of heart and he was troubled by it. He spoke his mind to the King. 'Please listen to my words, O King. Before you came to your father, King Bhumichandran, this country suffered a drought for twelve years. The famine was so severe that mothers were known to eat what little they found themselves, without sharing it with their children. You came to us like a great gift. You came like the first rains after the cruel heat of the summer. Since that time, never have the rains failed, nor has the land stopped from yielding. Since your arrival, no creature living in this country has known what it is to be hungry. If you should ever leave us, your people will lament like young children forsaken by their mother. If you should give up your guardianship of this sorrowing world and seek your own salvation, you would not be true to the path of the Buddha, whose compassion and pity was always towards others and not to himself. Therefore I beg you to put aside the thoughts in your mind.'

Puniyarajan listened carefully to his minister's advice. Yet he would not be deterred from his wish to visit Manipallavam and at least to worship at the shrine there. So he promised faithfully to be away for no more than a month, and left strict instructions for the guardianship of his country and people during his absence. And so, arranging for a ship and its crew to be made ready as soon as possible, he set sail.

Manimekalai was waiting for him in Manipallavam. Her face lit up with joy when he came ashore. She led him around the island once. As they traced their steps along the sacred shore, washed by the sea waves, and lapped about by the pure flower laden breezes, the shrine appeared in front of their eyes.

With great reverence Puniyarajan went towards it, walked three times around it, and stood silently in front of it. At once he saw his past life as Aaputran, with sharpness and clarity, as if he were seeing his own face reflected back to him in the mirror that he held in his hand. Raising his hands in salutation to the goddess Chintadevi, he spoke out in her praise.

'I now understand my past, and my sorrow drops away from me. Goddess of the beautiful temple in the southern city of Madurai, I remember now. At midnight one rainy season, a crowd of people came to me, fainting with hunger. I could give them nothing, for I lived alone, sharing with others the food that I received by begging. Seeing my distress, you placed the Amudasurabhi in my hands, and said, "Child, don't be sad. Even if this whole kingdom is gripped by famine, this alms-bowl will never be empty."

162

'Lady of the heavenly beings! Radiant and bejewelled light! You who are knowledge itself, and granter of truth; who alone can remove the falsehoods to which the best of us is prone! I praise you and worship you in this life and in all my lives to come.'

The King then rose to his feet and went with Manimekalai in a south-westerly direction. They came to the shores of the lake Komugi. There Puniyarajan rested in the shade of a flowering *punnai* tree.

Divatilakai, the guardian deity of the island saw them there and hastened to greet them. 'Great one,' she said, addressing the King, 'I welcome you back, you who in a former life appeased the hunger of so many, giving them life restoring food. This is the very spot where nine merchants returned with their ships, in search of you. Not finding you here, they chose to fast unto death. Even now you can see their bones, their only mortal remains. Here, in the dappled shade of this very tree, buried under this sand which is always washed by the ocean waves, you will find the cage of bones that once was the home of Aaputran's life. You chose to end that life as the nine merchants ended theirs. And now you, the very same, return here, a King.'

Divatilakai then turned to Manimekalai. 'Manimekalai, you who now carry the miraculous bowl in your hands, I have news for you. I must tell you that your great city Puhar now lies in the entrails of the sea. Let me tell you how this happened.'

'Pilivalai, the Naga princess who left the Chola King after living with him for a month, arrived at this island of Manipallavam with her baby, not so long ago. She walked around the island first, and then circled the shrine built by Indra, god of gods. At that moment, the trading ship of the merchant prince, Kambala Chetty, reached these shores. Pilivalai went up to the ship and enquired where it was bound. When she was told that it was on its return journey to Puhar, she handed her baby to Kambala Chetty saying, "This is the King's son. Take him to his father." The merchant was surprised, and then filled with great joy as he accepted his charge with reverence. But no sooner had they left the harbour and reached the high seas when a storm overtook them, overturning and splintering the ship.

'The few who survived the wreck eventually reached Puhar and hastened to tell the Chola King, Killivalavan of the unfailing spear, about the loss of the child. The King was utterly devastated. He mourned like a cobra that had lost its head jewel, forgetting all else and combing the shores and beaches of his land for his son. So it came about that he neglected to celebrate the Indra festival. Manimekalai Devi, of course, would not countenance the gross neglect. She cursed the jewelled city saying, "Let the ocean waves take it."

'At once the huge waves rose, spread over the city and swallowed it up. People fled in all directions. Nedumudi Killi had to save himself as best he could. But Manimekalai, the goddess of the seas, has asked me to tell you that the sage Aravana adigal has come to no harm whatsoever. Your mother and Sudhamati have gone with him to the city of Vanji.'

Divatilakai vanished, leaving Manimekalai to think about all that the sea had washed away, an entire history, buried deep in its entrails.

Meanwhile, Punyarajan looked about him. Then, with his bare hands he began to part the sand that stretched away beneath the *punnai* tree. Bones, bleached white and crumbling, appeared; the only evidence left of a body that was once breathing and sentient. Punyarajan was much moved by this visible proof of the passing of all things.

At once Manimekalai rose and came to him. She spoke very gently. 'Why do you looked so sad? Remember that you are a great King and that you wear the royal garland upon your chest even now. I sought you out in your island and brought you here only so that you might understand your former life. I only wish for you that your righteous reign may be an example throughout the four continents and the two thousand islands that surround them. If Kings renounce the world and give up governance, then justice will cease to have any meaning. Shall I tell you what dharma means, truly? It means nothing other than this : that you should feed, house and clothe all living beings. Never forget.'

The King said to her, 'I shall always try to do that much, both for the people of my own country, and for those who live in foreign lands. But to you I owe so much. You made it possible for me to see into my former life. It is as if you have created me anew. I cannot bear to leave you, nor to go away from this precious place.'

'Do not grieve', Manimekalai said, and she smiled. 'Your own people, sorrowing over your absence are calling you to come home. Listen. Can you not hear their beseeching voices? Go now to your waiting ship. I am bound for Vanji.' And so saying, she rose up into the skies.

19

The Pattini Goddess of Vanji

Swiftly Manimekalai flew through the skies and arrived at the gates of the great city of Vanji, capital of the Cheras. Once there, she immediately went to the temple. She wanted so much to see the images raised to her parents — Kannagi, who never failed in her love, and Kovalan, the generous-hearted. She stood in front of the images for a long time, remembering their many good qualities and mourning their tragic end. Then, weeping, she asked Kannagi, 'Tell me the reasons for what you did. Let me understand. You chose neither the path of penances as a widow, nor death at the funeral pyre of your husband. You blazed another path. Did that make you happy?'

Kannagi was now the pattini goddess. Her clear features were marked out in gold upon the dark stone. She was bejewelled, and wore a high head dress. The arresting eyes looked out of that beautiful golden face. In the quiet of the temple, Kannagi spoke, 'Daughter, on that terrible day that I burnt down Madurai in my anger, the tutelary deity of that city, Madurapati, appeared to me. She assured me that the events that had happened in Madurai were but the consequences of our former births.

'The goddess said that it all happened long ago in the flower-filled land of Kalinga. At that time, the kings Vasu and Kumara were lords over Singapuram and Kapilapuram respectively, and they were locked in battle. No one dared approach within a distance of six *kavathams* of the battlefield. However, a young merchant and refugee, Sangaman, dared to cross over to Singapuram, where he began to sell his jewellery. There, one of the King's agents, Bharatan — who was many years later to be the Kovalan we knew — apprehended Sangaman, and brought him before the King, claiming that he was a spy. And that was how the innocent merchant Sangaman was wrongfully put to death. Sangaman's wife, Nili, wept and lamented and finally threw herself off a high cliff. Before she fell to her death, she cursed her husband's wrong-doer.

'The goddess told me that it was the evil that Kovalan had done in a former life that came to fruition in this one. Even so, it cannot be escaped that it was I who in my anger destroyed a flourishing city.

'Listen, Manimekalai, my child. Kovalan and I joined the celestial beings because of certain good deeds that we did in our lives. But that must come to an end. My anger and revenge were wrong and I cannot escape their consequence. The gods too, like all mortal beings, must negotiate the ocean of rebirth and suffer many lives and many deaths. 'In the generous kingdom of Magadha, the city of Kapilavastu shines like a tilaka on the forehead of a god. There the Buddha appeared like the sun, having fulfilled in countless previous births the ten perfections — Generosity, Morality, Renunciation, Wisdom, Energy, Forbearance, Truthfulness, Resolution, Goodwill and Equanimity. He received his enlightenment under the Bodhi tree. He preached the four great truths about the impermanence of all things. He taught us about the twelve *nidanas* or causes that make up the wheel of desire. He taught us the path to freedom from bondage to this cycle. There will come a time when the light of this knowledge will spread like rays throughout Chakkaravalam.

'Your father and I acquired merit by praying in the seven *viharas* of the city of Puhar, created by Indra and dedicated to the Buddha. Because of that, we will be privileged to listen to his teaching of Dharma with loving hearts. So one day we will be free of this cycle of birth and re—birth.

'Now, Manimekalai, you must enter this ancient city and learn the doctrines that are particular to all the different religions from the many *pandits* here. When it is clear to you why none of them is satisfactory, you will be ready to accept the scriptures enshrined in the Tipitaka.'

Kannagi, the pattini goddess was silent. After a while she resumed. 'Wait. Let me give you one word of advice. Because you are so young, and especially, because you are a woman, the learned men of this city might be unwilling to teach you the finer points of their doctrines. Therefore, Manimekalai, change your form.'

Manimekalai agreed, and Kannagi blessed her. Clear in her resolve now, Manimekalai parted from her other mother, as she always thought of Kannagi, and spoke the *mantra* that Manimekalai Devi had given her. She chose the form of a young man, a mendicant scholar, as most appropriate to her needs.

Inside the city walls of Vanji stood temples, shrines, parks, flower gardens and artificial pools, and meeting places where learned men

gave their discourses. And there lived the Chera whose thronging armies wore the *vanji* flower in their hair, and whose elephants were like the mountain ranges of his kingdom. It was this same Senguttuvan who had crossed the Ganga with his troops, his chariots and his horses, and who had conquered many northern princes. It was he who had brought the stone from the Himalaya mountains, carried upon the heads of the princes Kanaka and Vijaya, the very stone from which the images of Kovalan and Kannagi were carved. Cheran Senguttuvan now wore the golden flower, *vanji*, in his crown as a symbol of his victory.

Manimekalai entered the city named for the *vanji* flower. The time was ripe for her to live out the four great truths.

168

Manimekalai in Pursuit of Truth

She was now in the disguise of a mendicant scholar, anxious to be taught the philosophies and doctrines of all the religions of that time.

She began with the Vedic systems, and went first to the scholars then known as the *Pramana-vadis*, who believed that truth can only be established by logical proof. They taught her all they knew of what is believed to be the six sources of true knowledge and the three main ways of inference, the only creditable means of reasoning and judgement, as well as the most common fallacies or unsound judgement.

She spent many days, understanding all this. Then she went by turn to the worshippers of Shiva, Brahma and Vishnu, each of whom told her about the attributes and characteristics of these great gods. They told her about Shiva who is made up of the sun and moon and of the five elements, and who is present in the life of all things. They spoke of Brahma who created the universe out of the cosmic egg, and of Narayana who is as blue as the deepest seas. And so she came to the *Veda-vadis* to whom the Vedas themselves are supreme, without begining or end, and who spent their entire time reading the texts and pronouncing their precepts and rules correctly.

Although she had spent much time with these learned men, somehow her heart could not give assent to any of their teachings. Nothing she had heard so far meshed closely with her own life experience. So she went on her way once more and came to the *Ajivikas* and the *Jainas*.

A renowned follower of the *Ajivikas* taught her about the doctrines of their founder, Makkhali Gosala. All life, he said, was nothing but atoms which start from the five elements, and which are in constant flux. These must all progress duly through geological, botanical and zoological forms of life. And all human life must inevitably pass through the six *karmic* colours of black, dark blue, green, red, gold and white before they can leave the cycle of birth and rebirth. There can be no escape from this rigid law of life.

Turning away from her Ajivika teacher, Manimekalai went on to the Niganthas, eager to hear what they had to tell her about Jainism. The *Nigantha-vadis* told her that according to their teachers, Jainism consisted of ten main components : Dharmastikayam, that which helps the *jiva* in this progress; Adharmastikayam, that which enables

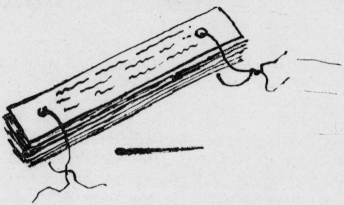

immobility; time and space; the faultless *jiva*; the invisible atom which is the base of all living things; good and bad deeds and their consequences; the bondage of the *jiva* and its release into moksha. Patiently, he went on to teach her about each of these things in detail.

She found both systems too rigid. Could it be that the great stream of her many lives was fixed in one determined path? She did not think so. She remembered what Kannagi had said about negotiating the ocean of births and rebirths. She thought of how she had to break free her life from that of Udayakumaran.

Passing on to the Sankhya and the Vaisesika pandits, at last she came to a *Bhuta-vadi*. The *Bhuta-vadis* held that the world is formed out of the five elements alone, without any divine intervention. We agree with the Lokayata, the sage said, and believe that when the elements combine together, a material body and a spirit come into existence. That is all. We believe that perception alone is our means of knowledge and nothing else. We recognise only one birth, and we know that our joys and pains end on earth with this one life.

Manimekalai smiled quietly, keeping to herself the vision she had been given in Manipallavam, still so vivid in her mind. She had spent a long time and had worked hard to understand all that these learned men had to say, so brilliantly and persuasively. Now she said to herself, 'Though what they say is quite clearly not what I recognise as Dharma, yet I shall not dispute with them.'

21

The Famine at Kanchi

It had been months now that she had lived as a young man, her mind given to the intricacies of argumentation. Now she was filled with a great yearning to see Madhavi and Sudhamati again, and to touch the feet of Aravana adigal once more. She knew it was time to move on. So she left the outer city where the pandits held their schools and came to the inner city and citadel of the Chera King.

The poet tells us that even the waters of river Vanji flowed with sweet-smelling unguents, incense and spices, washing over the fish and the crocodiles, and that the water's surface was thick with coloured lotus. The inner city walls were massive, and provided with a variety of devices for detecting and repelling enemies. Beyond the heavily guarded walls, the inner city streets were alive with people calling out their wares : all kinds of fish, sea salt, freshly drawn toddy, *pittu* and *appam*, meat, and the five aromatic spices. She passed the streets of goldsmiths and coppersmiths, of carpenters, sculptors and painters, of leather workers and tailors, makers of garlands, astrologers, musicians and bards. She passed a street where pearls were being strung. She passed the houses of the dancers and the separate street of the prostitutes. She marvelled at the weavers whose looms held many coloured threads, drawn so fine, the eye could hardly see them.

Nearest to the palace were the houses of the rich and the noble, the men who checked gold against a touchstone, the dealers in precious stones, the Brahmans, the ministers who advised the King, and others who held important positions in the city such as the commander of the army. She rejoiced to see the many temples and the public places where sermons and prayers were held.

Manimekalai walked along, light of heart, still in her disguise as a young man. She came at last to a famed monastery, beautiful as an Indra *vihara*, that is, created entirely out of Indra's mind alone. She was looking for Masattuvan, father of Kovalan, who had renounced the world after his son's tragedy.

Revealing herself to him, Manimekalai told her grandfather about the begging bowl in her hand, and about her recent visit to Manipallavam with King Puniyarajan of Java. She told him how the goddess of Manipallavam, Divatilakai, had informed her about the disaster at Puhar, from which Aravana adigal had brought her mother and Sudhamati into safety. She told him of her long discipline, the many days of listening to and learning from philosophical discourses. She was now ready, she said, for her final instructions and initiation at the hands of Aravana adigal.

'It is my good fortune and the outcome of my past good deeds that I see you now, Manimekalai,' said the old man. 'Listen to me, innocent one. When I heard of how your parents Kovalan and Kannagi died in such tragic circumstances, I suddenly came to understand the Lord Buddha's words about love and compassion. I was struck by the instability of this life, that of this earthly body that we experience; not so much as a grain of millet will last. That is why I chose the path of renunciation. But I must tell you why I chose to come to this city that bears the name of the *vanji* flower.

'Nine generations ago, it chanced that King Kudakko-cheral-adan was walking in these very gardens. He was a great Chera King who had the sign of his bow embossed upon the mountain sides as a token of his many victories. At the time that he was walking here, a certain Dharmacharana, a sage with divine powers, descended into the flower-laden park. This Dharmacharana was on his way back from Lanka where he had been on a pilgrimage to the holy mountain of Saman-oli. He came to rest on a small rock in front of the King. The Chera greeted the Charanar reverently and honoured him with food and refreshment. The sage, for his part, spoke to the King of the four noble truths of the Lord Buddha, and the way to rid oneself of the sorrow of birth.

'Now, I must tell you that Kudakko-cheral-adan had a great friend, Kovalan, who was at his side . This man was none other than a forefather of yours, nine generations preceding your father, and my son, the Kovalan we knew. The word of the Charanar made a deep impression on his mind. Now, our forefather was a rich man who had both inherited wealth and earned it himself. Yet within seven days he gave it all away, and built a *chaitya* for the Buddha upon the mountains here.

'I came to these parts because I longed to see this famous *chaitya* built by our forefather, and to worship here. Since I came here, I have

172

heard how Puhar, our beloved city, has been washed away by the sea. So, I have decided to stay here for the rest of my life.

'But, Manimekalai, Aravana adigal told me some days ago that the Oracle of the Pillar, Tuvatikan of Puhar, has discussed with you many events of your past lives. He also told me that the time had come for your last instructions and that you must receive them from him in the city of Kanchi. He has already gone there, accompanied by Madhavi and Sudhamati.

'There is one last thing that I must tell you. Kanchipuram, famous for its golden walls, is now laid waste. Its people suffer from drought and famine. You can see for yourself the multitudes of sufferers who left that city and have come as refugees to Vanji. Make it your duty, therefore, to go to that city like a rainbearing cloud, bringing food and comfort to the poor people who live there.'

Manimekalai bowed low to her grandfather and begged his permission to go. Then, bearing the divine alms-bowl in her hands, she rose high above the ancient city of Vanji with its massive walls hung about with Chera flags. From the west coast, she flew northwards to Kanchi.

Kanchi, in those days, was famous for its beauty, often compared with the divine city of Amravati where god Indra himself reigned. But when she drew nearer and saw the streets deserted, the people drawn-looking and half starved, her heart was wrung with pity. She flew once round the city walls in salutation, and then came down by the city centre. Then she went directly to the *chaitya* built by King Ilangkilli and dedicated to the Buddha.

One of the ministers of the state saw her in the park surrounding the *chaitya* and recognised her by the miraculous bowl that she carried. He hastened to bring the news to the King. 'I feel certain that this newcomer disguised as a mendicant is none other than the daughter of Kovalan. She is said to have renounced the world and is said to bear in her hands the miraculous Amudasurabi,' he said. 'Her arrival is a blessing; it is almost as if the rains have come.'

Eagerly the King set off with his court to the place where Manimekalai had been seen. 'Welcome to this city', he said to her. 'We know of your many good deeds of charity. You find us in the midst of a terrible drought. I have been in great anguish, not knowing why my people have had to suffer so. I asked myself whether it was a failure of justice on my part, or whether our holy men failed in their penances, or yet again, whether our women have led unchaste lives. As I was questioning myself sometime ago, a god appeared in front of me and comforted me. He told me that a young woman with a miraculous bowl would appear to us soon, and would save many lives, feeding the hungry. By her grace, he said, god Indra would summon the dark clouds and cause them to yield their rain plentifully. He went on to say that after the arrival of this young woman, there would never again be a drought in this land. Finally the god commanded me to create a park and lake in this city, exactly like the Komugi of Manipallavam with its surrounding gardens.

'I did as I was asked, in readiness for your arrival. Let me lead you there.'

Manimekalai walked about the newly laid gardens, delighting in what she saw, so reminiscent of her beloved island of peace, Manipallavam. Then she helped the King to design a replica of the shrine bearing the imprint of the lotus feet of the Enlightened One, and guarded by representations of the two goddesses, Divatilakai and Manimekalai Devi. At last she worshipped at the shrine, and placed the alms-bowl that she always carried, in front of it.

Then she called out in loud, clear tones, inviting all those who were in need, to come and eat. She summoned the blind, the deaf and the lame; all those who were left orphaned, or without shelter or clothes; all the sick and hungry; indeed all living creatures.

The alms-bowl produced food for all who came, like seed that is sown in good land and in due season, and which yields abundant harvest. At last, every one had eaten and had left, thanking Manimekalai and praising her.

It was not until she had accomplished this task that Aravana adigal came to her, accompanied by Madhavi and Sudhamati. Rejoicing to see them after such a long time, Manimekalai welcomed them, and tended to their needs, washing their feet and serving them with her own hands. After they had eaten and rested, she offered them betel leaves. Then at long last, she cast off the disguise that she had assumed for days and months, and returned to her own familiar form.

174

Aravana adigal listened to Manimekalai's account of all that had happened to her from the time she left Puhar and Queen Seerthi's palace. She told him of all that she had studied and learnt at Vanji, and how nothing that she had heard satisfied her spiritual yearning. The old man told her that she must always think and judge for herself. He said that there were only two unfailing modes of proof, *pratyaksha* — perception; and *anumana* — inference. Using these, she would learn to sift out the truth and stand steadfast by that, rejecting what was untrue.

22
The Last Journey

The time had come. She was ready for her initiation. Manimekalai looked back over the past months. What a long, long journey it had been since she sat stringing flowers for worship and listening to Madhavi tell the story of her parents' tragedy. Since then she had been granted insights into her previous lives; she had undertaken a mission to feed the hungry; she had chosen to base her life on the *silas*, the rules of morality. She had encountered Udayakumaran with such tragic results. Now at last she was ready for the next step. She dedicated herself in mind, body and word to the three jewels — the Buddha, the sangha and the dharma. She accepted these three as her sole refuge.

Aravana adigal blessed her tenderly. He had watched over her all this time, directing and guiding her steps towards this important moment. Now his words to her summed up all he could tell her about the path of the Buddha.

First he reminded her how the Buddha left the Tushita heavens because he was entreated by the gods to appear in the mortal world. Doing so as Siddhartha, the Sakya prince, he received his enlightenment in Gaya under the *Bodhi* tree. He was victorious over Mara, the evil one. He taught people how to be rid of greed, anger and delusion; he spoke words of truth and comfort to all living creatures. After his death, his many followers formed the sangha through which his words and teachings have been passed down through the centuries.

Once again, Aravana adigal reminded Manimekalai of the four noble truths — that all existence is full of sorrow, but that this sorrow has a cause, which therefore can be brought to an end, by following the eight-fold noble path. He told her again to avoid all evil, but to stand steadfast in the eightfold path of right view, right resolve, right speech, right action, right livelihood, right effort, right mindfulness and right concentration.

Once again he spoke to her of the wheel of cause and effect with its twelve linked stages, beginning with ignorance and ending with rebirth. By turn he explained each stage or *nidana*, and explained how each is linked or welded to the one before it and the one after. Therefore, he said, it is inevitable that ignorance must end in rebirth, and the experience of disease, old age and death. And just as one cause must have a certain result, the destruction of that cause must also remove the result. And so, working backwards, the destruction of ignorance must destroy, at last, the entire chain, ending all sorrow.

'Dear child', he said, 'remember always that ignorance is lack of awareness of the four noble truths and the cycle of twelve *nidanas*. Ignorance is delusion; it is the refusal to accept the evidence of one's own perception and experiences. It is like asking someone else whether a rabbit has horns, and simply accepting their answer, even if they say yes.'

He spoke at last of the three flaws — desire, hatred and delusion which are the root cause of sorrow. 'No one but you alone can choose either the cycle of attachment or liberation from it. There is no one else, however dear to you, who may share in that. You have learnt that lesson painfully and bitterly. Therefore, Manimekalai, remove desire by thinking about the impermanence of all things, their lack of essence. Do not mistake the painful or the inauspicious for that which it is not. Cast away hatred from your heart and mind by cultivating thoughts of friendship and compassion, and by learning to participate in the happiness of others. And finally, put an end to delusion by listening only to what is true and by reflecting upon that. So at last may you see all things as they are; with clearsightedness and with equanimity. Go forward bravely, and go alone.'

Aravana adigal blessed Manimekalai. She bowed low and said, touching his feet, 'Your words will be as a torch of wisdom to guide me on the path that I tread henceforth.'

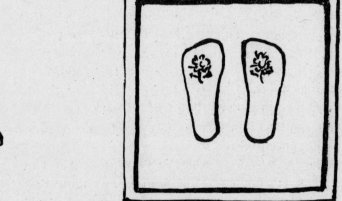

23
Afterword

The earliest Tamil poetry that has come down to us is usually called Sangam poetry, after the Sangam or academy of letters centred in Madurai. Traditionally it is held to be the last of three such Sangams. Sangam poetry has been collected into eight anthologies which consist of a number of poems of varying lengths, grouped under the two great themes of *aham* (love) and *puram* (war). These lyrics are largely secular and draw upon a complex, sophisticated poetic convention, which divides the Tamil country into five regions or landscapes — the mountains, wastelands, forest, cultivated plains and the coast. Each region is linked to an aspect of love and an attribute of war. Sangam poetry is full of vignettes, fragments of love stories, marvellous scenes in dialogue. But for the fully structured narrative we must look to *Silappadikaram* and *Manimekalai*.

Traditionally, these two poems have been described as *kappiyam*, and are part of a set of five. Of the other three — *Jivakachintamani*, *Valaiyapati*, and *Kundalakesi* — only the first is now extant. Using a variety of internal evidence, scholars tend to date the two poems *Silappadikaram* and *Manimekalai* at the fifth or sixth centuries of the common era, that is, a little later than Sangam times. The Tamil country described in them is very much that of the Sangam age, but with one striking difference, their Buddhist and Jaina messages of liberation from the chain of rebirth.

The Tamil country of the Sangam age is bounded by the Venkadam hills in the north and Kumari in the south. This whole area was divided into three ancient kingdoms — Chola towards the east of the peninsula, Pandya to the south, and Chera, modern Kerala, to the west. Each kingdom was named for the dynasty that ruled over it, and the three capitals were at Puhar, Madurai and Vanji. Besides the three crowned kings, *mudi-udai-vendar*, there were several independent chieftains acknowledging their overlordship. Some are praised in the early poems for their valour, their generosity towards poets and bards, and for the richness and beauty of their small states. One of the interesting features of *Silappadikaram*, in particular, is the vivid account it gives of the variety of life styles in the Tamil country — not only the differences between the three kingdoms, but also between sophisticated urban life within the ancient walled cities and the small peasant villages outside, and again between peasants along the river valley, the hill people and the forest tribes. *Manimekalai* extends this picture to include the dangerous sea routes to South East Asia.

Silappadikaram and *Manimekalai* have always been known as parallel poems. Tradition has it that the two poets, Ilanko adigal, younger brother of the Chera King Senguttuvan, and Sattanar, the grain merchant from Madurai, were friends and contemporaries. The *patikam* or prefaces to the two poems refer to the fact that the two works were composed in parallel by the two poets, and first recited to each other.

The story material of the two poems is the same. The story of Kovalan and Kannagi is one of the oldest legends of the Tamil country, and also of Sri Lanka; different versions of it have come down to us, though Ilanko's version is the best known. *Manimekalai* is meant to be a sequel to *Silappadikaram*, being the story of the renunciation of Kovalan's and Madhavi's daughter. It also makes close references to many of the events, characters and places which are mentioned in the first poem. At the same time, it is also, importantly, a re-working of the story in Buddhist terms. Besides many inter-textual references, there are also echoes in the second work, of motifs from the first — the centrality of the Indra festival, for instance; the presence of the goddess Manimekalai who has jurisdiction over seas and storms; the two tragic deaths, both happening in temples, and each being the result of a fatal mistake.

But perhaps what is most striking for the modern reader is that the central characters in both poems are women — Kannagi, Madhavi, Kavundi adigal and Manimekalai. These are women who make unusual choices, out of line with conventional heroines. They move out of the available literary stereotypes of wife, mistress and renunciant, re-interpreting each of these roles.

Silappadikaram tells of the transformation of Kannagi from the role of faithful and dutiful wife to single-minded avenger of the wrong done to her husband. She deliberately chooses against the other two options available to her — death upon her husband's funeral pyre or a continuing life of penances as a widow. Although there is a second transformation of her as a goddess, what is unforgettable in the poem is the description of her, consumed by rage

178

as she denounces the King and flings her blazing breast upon Madurai.

Madhavi, too, steps out of line from her given role. Following her seven years of training in song and dance, and then her debut performance in the presence of the King, she achieves a particular status in the city of Puhar, symbolised by her yearly performances at the prestigious Indra festival. But just as she is prepared to give up Kovalan with dignity, she also relinquishes this role, going directly against the traditions of her community, and disregarding the disapproval of the elders of the city.

Ilanko describes Kavundi, the Jain renunciant, with considerable insight and knowledge. From the earliest times of Mahavira there were Jain monastic orders for men and women. Jain canons give a full account of the monastic life which one could enter as young as seven and a half years. A novice had her head shaved — indeed the individual hairs were pulled out — and renounced all her possesions. Thenceforth she carried only the equipment of a renunciant: an alms-bowl, a water pot, a bundle of peacock feathers and the strips of cloth that covered her. She became a full member of the monastic community after a novitiate of about four months, by taking the five great vows — never to injure living things, to speak the truth always, to refrain from stealing, to refrain from any sexual activity, and not to possess any property.

There are precise rules governing the day-to-day life of those who have renounced the world. In the rainy season, that is for four months of the year, they may stay in one place, a dwelling they have got by begging and which is not used by the owner, his family, his servants or his cattle. These were originally isolated places, later community houses sprang up where the lay people gathered to hear sermons and explanations of the scriptural texts. For the rest of the year they must travel constantly; they may not stay longer than three nights in a village and five nights in a town. Each day and night is divided into four parts with set times for meditation, private study, travel and collecting alms and sleep. It was a life of extreme austerity, sometimes ending in voluntary starvation, an accepted mode of death.

Ilanko's intriguing portrayal of Kavundi who seems to live largely as a recluse, fills out and makes credible the stark picture we get of the monastic life from rules for the monks and nuns. For Kavundi is formidably stern and austere, but as well as this, she shows an extraordinary and unexpected flow of sympathy towards her 'children' as she comes to call Kovalan and Kannagi. She is human enough to become enmeshed in their tragedy which emphasises the terrible lesson of the inevitability of fate.

Perhaps the most intriguing portrait out of the four women is that of Manimekalai. In her case, most poignantly, the human motives of love and affection, perfected over many lives, pull her in one direction, while the quest for spiritual liberation pulls her in another. It is only when this is resolved that her spiritual journey can go ahead. Then, we are never allowed to forget that Manimekalai — unlike Kavundi adigal in the previous poem — is young and beautiful. This in itself serves as a commentary to the message that is repeated throughout the poem, of the passing of all things, particularly youth and beauty. Further, her grandmother, Chitrapati, eldest of the female line, repeatedly reminds us that the girl belongs to the community of dancers and therefore, renunciation is not an option that is available to her. It is against all this that Manimekalai struggles to justify her choice as a renunciant. As with Kannagi and Kavundi, we see a development of her character through the poem. She who finds it so difficult to communicate her message of detachment to Udayakumaran, learns to part from Puniyarajan with wisdom and compassion. A number of paradoxes are resolved in the character of Manimekalai — love and renunciation; alms-giving and alms-receiving; even at one point, male and female.

Despite much that is common or complementary between the two poems, however, there are also some striking differences. Each poem, besides the prefaces, contains thirty subdivisions or *kadai*. However, whereas in *Manimekalai* the *kadai* are not grouped in any way, *Silappadikaram* sets them out under three *kandam*, each named for the capital of one of the three great kingdoms, Puhar, Madurai and Vanji. Again, while *Manimekalai* follows a fairly simple style and verse metre throughout, several of the subsections in *Silappadikaram* are made up almost entirely of song sequences. The tone of *Manimekalai* tends to be serene, though sometimes necessarily sombre and didactic, and at other times — as in the beautiful prayers embedded in it — rising to a note of pure devotion. *Silappadikaram* is altogether more dramatic, particularly in the wonderful Madurai section. Perhaps a main structural difference is in the fact that *Silappadikaram* on the whole tells a linear story, whereas *Manimekalai* adopts the complex mode of binding together a number of *kilai kadai* or branch stories. Manimekalai's own story loops backwards and forwards, revealing a direction that is perfected over many, many births.

180

Thematically, too, the two poems are strikingly different. The preface to *Silappadikaram* tells us that the story illustrates three truths — that Kings who deviate from the path of *aram*, righteousness, will cause their own destruction; that chastity and steadfastness are admired by the truly great; and that all of us must necessarily bear the consequences of past deeds.

The first theme is made clear through the symbolism of the royal insignia, particularly the sceptre, *kol*, literally a rod or staff; and the royal white umbrella, *ven-korra-kudai*. The *kol* stands for royal justice, by its straightness the King's rule is to be judged. The umbrella stands for the King's mercy towards his subjects. The invocation to *Silappadikaram* begins with three stanzas in praise of the moon, sun and clouds, in which the moon is compared with the cool white umbrella of the Chola King, protecting and shading his people. When the King loses his attributes of mercy and clemency, the high-held umbrella is said to be lowered.

The central theme of chastity and steadfastness is illustrated by Kannagi's story, and the third, by the poem's general tenor.

According to popular tradition, Ilanko was a Jain, and we have no reason to doubt this. Now the world according to the Jains is neither created, maintained nor destroyed by the intervention of a personal god; it functions only according to an unalterable and eternal law. Belief in karman, *ul-vinai* in Tamil, is the pivot of Jain ethics. All actions carry their own rewards or punishment, either in this world or in the world to come. So it is by one's own effort alone that one may escape the wheel of birth and rebirth.

This message is strongly stressed in *Silappadikaram*, but not only by the Jain ascetic whom the travellers meet on the way to Uraiyur, but also by the holy woman and renunciant, Kavundi adigal, and by the author himself speaking directly at the end of the poem; Madalan the Brahman and the guardian deity of Madurai bring it out as well. This view of the world provides the framework for the story and the solution to Kovalan's and Kannagi's tragedy.

But whereas *Silappadikaram* has several themes and gives space to different religious perspectives, *Manimekalai* has a single unifying theme — Manimekalai's spiritual journey and its justification. It is entirely Buddhist in its purpose. It is perhaps important to remember that it is the only extant Tamil Buddhist poem, that it suffered gross neglect for many years, and was only re-discovered in the late nineteenth century by the efforts of the brilliant scholar, Dr U. V. Swaminathaiyar. It is therefore unique in combining Tamil literary conventions with pan-Indian Buddhist story elements. For example, the motif of the courtesan appears several times in Buddhist texts to illustrate the transience of beauty; it is perhaps best known in a verse from the *Therigatha*, attributed to Ambapali. The Goddess Manimekalai Devi, guardian of the seas is a familiar figure in many Jataka tales. And the story of Gotamai and her dead child is one more version of Gotamai and the mustard seed, perhaps the best known of all Buddhist stories. The poem is full of references to the fabulous islands of the South East, and Buddhist relics there. At the same time, it is imbued with the symbolism of life as an ocean of sorrow, to be crossed with difficulty by holding on to the raft of knowledge. The Tamil story of a young woman who chooses to become a *bhikkuni* and the charting of her spiritual endeavour is particularly startling because there is neither a Buddhist community left in the Tamil country, nor usually an order of women renunciants in countries that follow the Theravada tradition.

If *Manimekalai* is unique in giving us an insight into early Tamil Buddhism, *Silappadikaram* is one of the few texts which gives us information about the now extinct *yaal*, a hand-held harp which preceded the veena, and about the early South Indian systems of music and dance. The two poems together give us many vivid insights into the life of the times —of thriving townships, of contact with the west through the Yavanas, and of trade routes to the east, of the scholasticism of Vanji and of Buddhist centres such as Kanchi. We see that many Vedic rituals have been absorbed into the life of the Tamil country, both in the domestic sphere, for example, the wedding rites of Kovalan and Kannagi, and in the public sphere as in the Rajasuya *yajna* which Cheran Senguttuvan undertakes. But along with this the local deities flourish, there are popular mythologies of spirits and demons, and there are many rituals specific to tribes and villages. The old Tamil god Murugan and the war-goddess Korravai are worshipped with dances and processions. Of particular interest are the vividly described figures of Aiyai, goddess of the hunters, and Madurapati, guardian of the city of Madurai.

We are fortunate, then, in having these two poems, both for their historical interest and for the boldness and complexity of their literary design. But most of all, they speak to us with immediacy, telling their powerful stories of remarkable women who made such remarkable choices in their time.

182

Notes on some colour plates

The Wedding of Kannagi and Kovalan (facing page 6) : The background colour as well as the clothes worn by the bride and groom are yellow which traditionally represents auspiciousness. The mounted pots and the plantain stems are additional symbols of prosperity.

The Journey (facing page 28) : The sombre shades of this painting mark the mood of this scene. In addition, the finer details–the buffalo in the swamp, the egrets waiting to pick on the insects, the crows, the bare walls of the houses and Kavundi adigal's white-grey cloth–are a grim pointer to the change that will come into the couple's lives.

Kannagi Breaks the Silambu (facing page 68) : The intensity of the scene is captured in the depth of the colours. Note especially the white umbrella, standing for the reputation of the king as a protector of the people, now bent, and the *kol* (sceptre) now fallen. The shame and guilt is evident in the bent heads of all present: Kannagi alone holds her head upright.

Madurai in Flames (facing page 72) : The power of the flames is conveyed by their overwhelming prominence while the insignificance of the human beings is marked by their minuteness and the need to search them out in the melee. In the foreground the Gods of Madurai are seen abandoning the city with calm detachment.

Senguttuvan's Expedition (facing page 86) : The violence the chaos that ironically becomes a part of the expedition to build a temple dedicated to Kannagi, is evident in the breadth of lines and the concentrated action in the painting.

Uvavana (facing page 100) : The lines and curves in this picture are deliberately unrealistic since the garden is a refuge from the grim reality pursuing Manimekalai in the form of Prince Udayakumaran. Note the sense of depth and peace conveyed by the shades of green.

Chakkaravala Kottam (facing page 110) : Note the hills in the foreground symbolising the seven heavens and the evolution of the being through successive births till nirvana is attained.

Manimekalai's Vision (facing page 116) : Buddha, here seen in abhaya mudra, is central to *Manimekalai*. The vast use of shades of white conveys a sense of tranquility and detachment. The painting is remarkably uncluttered.

The First Alms (facing page 132) : A traditional village house. The painting captures the many details of the rural ambience.

Notes on some chapter symbols

Silappadikaram

The silambu or the anklet is central to the story. The text describes Kannagi's silambu as being made of gold, its colour tinged with the green-gold of the parrot's wing. Note the detail in the artist's representation of the silambu, especially the parrots placed as part of the pattern.

Chapter 1: *A Wedding in Puhar*
The drums and the pipe herald joy and happy events.

Chapter 4: *The Anklet*
The temple towers in the city of Madurai are central to this chapter though it is titled *The Anklet*.

Chapter 5: *Kannagi in Madurai*
The royal throne and the white umbrella are symbols of promised protection. These are cruelly denied to Kannagi and all Madurai has to pay the price for it.

Manimekalai

The theme of this story is one of the renunciation and detachment, and the alms bowl is strongly representative of this. The bowl is also the Amudasurabi which figures centrally in the text. It sates the many who strive for physical and spiritual fulfilment.

Chapter 1: *Manimekalai, Another Beginning*
The Indra festival that is so much a part of Puhar, is the most obvious link between this text and *Silappadikaram*. The festival later becomes the reason for the destruction of Puhar.

Chapter 3: *The Crystal Pavilion*
The attempts of Udayakumaran to woo Manimekalai that constitute the essence of this chapter, are represented by the symbol of Kama, the God of Love, armed with his sugarcane-bow and flower-tipped arrows.

Chapter 4: *The Story of Chakkaravala Kottam*
Stylistically representing the hands in a benevolent gesture conveying the peace that oneness with Buddha promises. The hands can also be seen as doves, a symbol of peace.

Chapter 11: *Kayachandikai*
The eternally burning fire here represents the curse of unending hunger that Kayachandikai burdens under — *yaanaiti* or elephant-fire.

Chapter 15: *Aftermath*
The pair of scales appropriately signify that the time for weighing consequences and for reconciling cause and effect has arrived.

Chapter 18: *Puniyarajan's Pilgrimage*
Puniyarajan's quest for Truth is aptly signified by the series of telescopic doors stretching into eternity.

Glossary

aati flower: the flower of the mountain ebony, symbol of the Cholas

adigal: a term of respect used along with names of sages and ascetics, both male and female

aham: that which is the inner; one of the two divisions of early Tamil literature, consisting of all the poetry that deals with the theme of love and family relationships.

ajivika: a follower of Makkali Goṣala, a contemporary of Mahavira and of Buddha, who taught a view of the universe in which all beings are linked in an inevitable and unalterable process of bondage, evolution and release

anumana: deduction or critical reasoning

appam: small cakes of rice flour, savoury or sweet eaten fried or steamed.

arivan: he who has attained knowledge or wisdom; here also Mahavira, the last of the Tirthankaras, and commonly held to be the founder of Jainism

asura: a class of demons, enemies of the gods

bhikkuni: a female Buddhist ascetic, one who has renounced the world to follow the path of Buddha

Bhuta-vadi: from bhuta, meaning element; believers in the existence only of the physical elements; absolute materialists

bhutam: genie; a mythical creature often associated with a particular place

chaitya: a buddhist shrine attached to a stupa. Stupas were originally burial mounds containing relics of the Buddha.

dharma: truth, law, principle of righteousness; also the doctrine of the Buddha

gandharva: a form of marriage based on mutual love alone, and without the performance of any ritual

Jaina: a follower of the religion founded by Vardhamana Mahavira (Jina), a contemporary of the Buddha, and supposedly the last of 24 Tirthankaras or liberators. Jainas practise a strict code of morality, with great emphasis on non-violence, and believe in the perfectibility of the self.

jiva: in Jainism, the aggregate of a number of distinct life-units or atoms. These are all essentially alike, but become tainted to different degrees by contact with time, space and matter, all aspects of ajiva; salvation lies in the dissolution of this combination.

kadai: a self-contained sub-section of a long narrative poem

kalanju: a weight, equal to about one sixth of an ounce, used for measuring gold

kama: the God of Love, armed with a bow of sugarcane whose bowstring is a line of bees, and whose arrows are each tipped with a distinct flower

kanal vari: love songs of fisherfolk, sung along the coastal regions

kanchi blossom: a riverside flower, worn as garlands by soldiers

kandam: a main division of a long narrative poem, often containing several kadai or sub-sections. *Silappadikaram* has three main kandams, named for Puhar, Madurai and Vanji, each of which contain differently named kadai.

kappiyam: a Tamil narrative poem, dealing with the four themes of aram (righteousness), porul (worldly success), inbam (pleasure), and vidu (release)

karma: action, conduct; action with inevitable consequences; the moral law of cause and effect in all human activities

kavatham: a distance of about ten miles

kilichirai: gold resembling the parrot's wing; said to be one of four kinds of gold

koel: sometimes called the Indian cuckoo, a bird with a hauntingly beautiful call

kol: sceptre; symbol of royalty, and of uprightness and justice

kottam: enclosed space; used also in *Silappadikaram* and *Manimekalai* to mean a monastery or a temple enclosure

kumkum: an auspicious mark, worn on the forehead

kuravai: a particular kind of dance in a circle, performed by women in ancient times, and associated with hillside and woodland regions

mantra: magical formula or incantation

marutam: See note to *mullai*. Marutam is a red flower growing near water, is associated with pastoral regions overseen by Vendan (Indra), and stands for unfaithfulness in love.

moksha: liberation from bondage

mullai: one of the five landscapes of early Tamil poetics, the others being kurinji, marutam, neytal and palai. Each stands for a mood or feeling, is associated with a region presided over by a deity, and represented by a flower. Thus mullai, the jasmine flower, is associated with the forest region overseen by Mayan (Vishnu), and signifies patient waiting.

naaval fruit: A sweet, dark-skinned fruit; the jamun-plum

Nala and Damayanti: this story is one of the episodes of *Mahabharata*. Damayanti chooses Nala for her husband at a swayamvara or formal gathering of royal suitors at which there were four gods who had assumed his likeness. They marry and live in great happiness until one day Nala loses everything he possesses to his younger brother Pushkara with whom he plays a game of dice. They leave for the forest, where, in the middle of the night, Nala divides the single garment upon which they are lying, and abandons Damayanti in the hope that she at least will return to her father's court. After much suffering they are reunited and at last regain their lost kingdom.

Nigantha-vadi: followers of Nigantha, the philosophical theory of Jainas

nirvana: cessation of ignorance and desire; the attainment of a pure and peaceful realm of mind; the realisation of enlightenment

pandits: scholars and teachers

patikam: preface, introduction or foreword

pittu: steamed rice-flour food, sweetened or spiced

Pramana-vadi: logician

pratyaksha: direct perception

punnai: a small tree with shiny dark green leaves and little white flowers; mastwood

nidanas: the twelve links in the chain of causation (ignorance, will to action, consciousness, psycho-physical existence, sense organs, contact of subject and object, feeling, desire, grasping, birth, decay and death).These are shown as the wheel of life in Buddhist art.

puram: that which is outside, the external. One of the two divisions of early Tamil literature, consisting of all the poetry that deals with themes of war, kingship and heroism

rajasuya yajna: a great sacrifice performed at the installation of a king, religious in nature, but also political in intent. It implied that he who instituted the sacrifice was a supreme lord, and his tributary princes were required to be present at the rite.

Rati: wife of Kama, God of Love

sadhvi: a female ascetic

sila: the five Buddhist rules of good conduct or morality: not to kill, not to steal, not to commit any sexual misconduct, not to lie, not to take any intoxicant

Tirumal: another name of the god Vishnu

tulasi: the sacred basil plant

Vaikasi: the second Tamil month, May to June. The full-moon day of Vaikasi is said to be the day of the birth, the Enlightenment and the passing away of the Buddha, and is celebrated as the most important day for all Buddhists.

vanji flower: the flower of the palm tree and emblem of Chera kings

varna: four-fold divisions of society into brahman, kshatriya, vaishya and shudra

Vasuki: King of the Nagas, used by the gods and asuras as a coil around the mountain Mandara when they churned the ocean

Veda-vadi: a member of a sect for whom no other divinity existed other than the sacred text of the Vedas

vidyadhara: A class of celestial beings inhabiting the regions betwen earth and sky, and generally of a benevolent disposition

vihara: a Buddhist monastery, later also used as a place of worship

Wheel of Dharma: when the Buddha preached his first sermon in the deer park of Sarnath, he is said to have set in motion the Dhammachakka (Dharmachakra) or the wheel of righteousness.

yaal: an ancient muscial instrument, supposed to have been like a hand-held harp

yaanaiti: literally, elephant-fire; here used to mean an insatiable hunger

yojana: said to be a distance of about three miles